I Never Knew You

I Never Knew You

✦

Why do you call me, "Lord, Lord", and do not do what I say?

John R. Singleton

iUniverse, Inc.
New York Lincoln Shanghai

I Never Knew You
Why do you call me, "Lord, Lord", and do not do what I say?

iUniverse books may be ordered through booksellers or by contacting:

iUniverse
2021 Pine Lake Road, Suite 100
Lincoln, NE 68512
www.iuniverse.com
1-800-Authors (1-800-288-4677)

ISBN-13: 978-0-595-35154-1 (pbk)
ISBN-13: 978-0-595-79855-1 (ebk)
ISBN-10: 0-595-35154-9 (pbk)
ISBN-10: 0-595-79855-1 (ebk)

Printed in the United States of America

Contents

Acknowledgements

I'd like to thank my wife for being a patient sounding board for the past 29 years. Very few people could continue to listen to the same theme repeated dozens of times. I also appreciate the sound preaching and teaching of pastors like Lee Shipp, Rusty Tardo and Ray Wells.

Foreword

I'll be the first to admit I'm a skeptic, and I tend to believe there are three basic types of people in this world: optimists, pessimists, and realists. I'm a realist, and in the process of wearing that label, people often mistakenly decide I'm a pessimist. I guess it only stands to reason that anyone who does their best to see life as it really is might come across somewhat pessimistic. If there's a subject that draws out the true optimist, pessimist and realist nature in people, it has to be the topic of Salvation. I think most of us form our opinions about life's greatest subjects early in our lives, and after that we simply build a case for what we believe as we age.

I earnestly want to convey a solid, Biblical basis for what I believe about Salvation in this book. In the process of providing an honest viewpoint, I must point out a few things this book isn't. I don't provide Scriptural references or help to support any opposing views to what I believe. Why? The answer is simple—the vast majority of books and sermons on Salvation principles lean very clearly towards the concept of "Saved by Grace alone" and "All you must do to be saved is believe in Jesus Christ". These concepts don't need to be stated again, since most people have been bombarded by them their entire lives. Over the past 7 years I've written and spoken on the topic of "True Salvation" and have made a simple offer to the readers and hearers of that message many times. The offer? For every Scriptural reference someone provides that says "Saved by Grace alone", or "All you must do to be saved is believe in Jesus Christ", I will send back two Scriptural references that say otherwise. It's of critical importance to understand I'm in no way minimizing either belief, rather I'm saying, without any reservations, that anyone who claims to be a Christian must be active in their Christianity.

The reader should appreciate something early on: It would make my life much easier to simply move over to "the other side" and accept the easy path to Salvation rather than the much tougher position I firmly adhere to. Ultimately, one must ask themselves one of two fundamental questions:

How <u>good must I be</u> to enter Heaven?
Or
How <u>bad can I be</u> and <u>still</u> enter Heaven?

Once again, for those who have been raised on "Saved by Grace alone", either question may seem ludicrous, but are they? I've been told that whenever I "question" the sacrifice of Jesus on the cross I'm insulting God. If that's true, I'm sorry, but when I consider how God might deal with me for wanting to "earn" my Salvation versus his treatment of those who trample on his Grace, I'll take my chances. If I can stand before God and say without reservation that I did indeed believe Jesus was his son, and I believe that Jesus <u>was</u> resurrected and <u>can</u> take away my sins, I think I'm fulfilling his expectations for me in terms of understanding his plan of Salvation. If there's anything I do worry about, it's the thought God will question why I persisted in many of the sins I commit. I don't know of a single person who doesn't have at least one sin they could stop committing with minimal effort.

I implore you to keep your Bible open as you read this book. Whenever you doubt the context of a Scriptural reference, look it up and read as much as you need to overcome that doubt. If you're a fan of Bible versions other than the New International Version, read what your Bible says within a given section of Scripture. If your version suggests I'm wrong, please let me know (<u>info@basicchristian.com</u>). By the way, I capitalize words like "Bible", "Heaven" and "Scripture" out of respect, whether it's considered proper or not.

Last, but certainly not least, I'd like to acknowledge there <u>are</u> some fine pastors out there. I believe the vast majority of preachers are ineffective, so if you've got a good pastor, you're very fortunate.

1

Repentance

✦

More than saying, "I'm sorry"

Repentance is a very consistent topic in the New Testament beginning with John the Baptist. John the Baptist is often pushed aside by pastors and teachers simply because little was written about this eccentric man. The most important thing to remember about John the Baptist is what <u>Jesus</u> said about him:

Matthew 11
¹¹ "I tell you the truth: Among those born of women there has not risen anyone greater than John the Baptist; yet he who is least in the kingdom of heaven is greater than he."

This passage certainly proves that Jesus held John the Baptist in high regard. Read it again and try to think of whom Jesus ever paid a higher complement. The Baptist's messages always featured the same basic theme: "Repent", and for Jesus to pay homage to this man, he was also paying homage to his message. Just how important was repentance to Jesus? Let's look at Jesus' first "official" words of instruction to the people:

Matthew 4
¹⁷From that time on Jesus began to preach, "Repent, for the kingdom of heaven is near."

Was this a fluke? Keep reading.

Mark 1
15 "The time has come," he said. "The kingdom of God is near. Repent and believe the good news!"

It's interesting that Jesus himself put repentance first and "believe the good news" second in his instructions above. Still not convinced that Jesus was "big on repentance"? Read on.

Luke 13
1Now there were some present at that time who told Jesus about the Galileans whose blood Pilate had mixed with their sacrifices. 2Jesus answered, "Do you think that these Galileans were worse sinners than all the other Galileans because they suffered this way? 3I tell you, no! But unless you repent, you too will all perish. 4Or those eighteen who died when the tower in Siloam fell on them — do you think they were more guilty than all the others living in Jerusalem? 5I tell you, no! But unless you repent, you too will all perish."

Jesus tells the crowd in verse three they must repent or perish. Just to be sure they heard him, he repeats the admonition again in verse five. These teachings of Jesus were clearly important to him, and should have become equally important to those who claim him as Savior. The act of repentance seems to confuse many people. The easy believism crowd would like to distract true believers by reminding them that "we can't work our way to Heaven—Jesus already paid for our sins". While it's very true we can't work our way to Heaven, we can certainly endanger our Salvation by not acting on the instructions of Jesus. Here's my favorite "practical" story of repentance:

Luke 19
1Jesus entered Jericho and was passing through. 2A man was there by the name of Zacchaeus; he was a chief tax collector and was wealthy. 3He wanted to see who Jesus was, but being a short man he could not, because of the crowd. 4So he ran ahead and climbed a sycamore-fig tree to see him, since Jesus was coming that way.
5When Jesus reached the spot, he looked up and said to him, "Zacchaeus, come down immediately. I must stay at your house today." 6So he came down at once and welcomed him gladly.

⁷All the people saw this and began to mutter, "He has gone to be the guest of a 'sinner.'"
⁸But Zacchaeus stood up and said to the Lord, "Look, Lord! Here and now I give half of my possessions to the poor, and if I have cheated anybody out of anything, I will pay back four times the amount."
⁹Jesus said to him, "Today salvation has come to this house, because this man, too, is a son of Abraham. ¹⁰For the Son of Man came to seek and to save what was lost."

Zacchaeus was much like people today who are searching for truth and answers to life's problems. I would tend to think a wealthy chief tax collector would have been embarrassed to climb a tree, but that shows how much Zacchaeus wanted to see Jesus. Zacchaeus is a great example of a man who voluntarily sacrificed to please the man he would claim as Lord. Many people today confuse confession of sin with repentance of sin, but the two are very distinct entities. Confession simply amounts to "I goofed up and I'm sorry", whereas repentance contains the confession <u>and</u> adds the next (and critical) level: <u>action</u>. What was Zacchaeus' action? Read the passage again—he wants to make amends by giving half of his possessions to the poor and going to the next step by saying if he has cheated anyone out of anything he will pay back four times the amount. Are we strong enough in our repentance to even come close to what Zacchaeus offered? Very few of us have made it into adulthood without cheating someone. Oh sure, you probably don't think you ever have, but unless you give your employer a full 40 hours of work for 40 hours of pay, you've cheated him. If you sold someone a used car and you didn't disclose a problem after the prospective buyer asked you specifically, "Is there anything wrong with the car?"; then you cheated him. I've probably cheated hundreds of people in my 50 years on this earth—sometimes intentional, sometimes accidental. I'll probably be making amends until the day I die, but I consider that to be part and parcel of my Salvation experience.

Luke 24
⁴⁵Then he opened their minds so they could understand the Scriptures. ⁴⁶He told them, "This is what is written: The Christ will suffer and rise from the dead on the third day, ⁴⁷and repentance and forgiveness of sins will be preached in his name to all nations, beginning at Jerusalem."

This meeting between Jesus and his Disciples happened <u>after</u> the resurrection, so the modern "Christian" movement had begun. How did Jesus kick-off the movement? Read it again: "**repentance and forgiveness of sins will be preached in his name…**" Repentance <u>was</u> important to Jesus. By the way, for all of those who like to confuse the Salvation process by teaching, "You really need to understand who Jesus was talking to at the time. Was it a Jewish audience or was it a Gentile audience?" This is simply another tactic to allow the easy believism teachers and preachers to mislead people into thinking that Jesus had unique messages for different categories of people. Jesus was very consistent in his teachings regardless of who the audience was. Is faith in God only to be taught to Jews? To Gentiles? Should only Gentiles repent? Let's get real here and agree that the basic message of Jesus Christ can't be customized for any specific group. How the various groups interpreted the words of Jesus can be the subject of debate, but the intent is the same for all people.

John 5
[13]**The man who was healed had no idea who it was, for Jesus had slipped away into the crowd that was there.**
[14]**Later Jesus found him at the temple and said to him, "See, you are well again. Stop sinning or something worse may happen to you."**

After Jesus healed the crippled man, what advice did Jesus give him before leaving? Stop sinning. Can we simply stop sinning? Of course not, but Jesus was putting the man on notice to get his life in order, and Jesus expects us to do the same. If a modern charlatan like Benny Hinn really could heal a crippled person, his next move would be to get him to "sow a seed of faith". What did Jesus want from the man? Money? Nope…"Stop sinning."

Acts 2
[38]**Peter replied, "Repent and be baptized, every one of you, in the name of Jesus Christ for the forgiveness of your sins. And you will receive the gift of the Holy Spirit."**

There have been and will continue to be arguments on what "be baptized" really means, but focus on what Peter listed first: "Repent". Peter learned from "the boss", Jesus, that repentance was important. I personally think that since Jesus didn't spend a lot of time talking about water baptism, he didn't consider it to be of critical importance. The folks from the Church of Christ won't be happy with that opinion, but I seriously doubt this book will make anyone happy anyway.

Acts 3
[19]**Repent, then, and turn to God, so that your sins may be wiped out, that times of refreshing may come from the Lord, [20]and that he may send the Christ, who has been appointed for you—even Jesus.**

Peter is addressing a crowd in the days and months <u>following</u> the crucifixion of Christ. What did he say? "Repent….so that your sins may be wiped out." But Peter is speaking, and we're continually reminded that the Apostle <u>Paul</u> is the man sent to us, the Gentiles. But wait….in this <u>same</u> book of Acts, <u>Paul</u> has some things to say about repentance.

Acts 17
[30]**In the past God overlooked such ignorance, but now he commands all people everywhere to repent.**

Acts 20
[21]**I have declared to both Jews and Greeks that they must turn to God in repentance and have faith in our Lord Jesus.**

Well, well, it seems that good old Paul is also a big believer in repentance. Notice the order in Acts 20:21: **"turn to God in repentance and have faith in our Lord Jesus."** I think you'll see a definite pattern of "repent and believe" if you'll take the time to look.

2 Corinthians 7
[8]**Even if I caused you sorrow by my letter, I do not regret it. Though I did regret it—I see that my letter hurt you, but only for a little while— [9]yet now I am happy, not because you were made sorry, but because your sorrow led you to repentance. For you became sorrowful as God intended and so were not harmed in any way by us. [10]Godly sorrow brings repentance that leads to salvation and leaves no regret, but worldly sorrow brings death.**

The trend in the modern church today is to avoid hurting anyone's feelings. This "I'm okay, you're okay" mentality is sending hundreds of thousands of people to Hell every year, but somehow we've decided that self-esteem is more important than an eternity in Heaven. Paul was much like a small group of dedicated preachers today—he didn't really want to hurt their feelings, but when he considered the alternative, he decided that hurt feelings were a minor inconvenience compared to an eternity in Hell.

2 Corinthians 12

²⁰For I am afraid that when I come I may not find you as I want you to be, and you may not find me as you want me to be. I fear that there may be quarreling, jealousy, outbursts of anger, factions, slander, gossip, arrogance and disorder. ²¹I am afraid that when I come again my God will humble me before you, and I will be grieved over many who have sinned earlier and have not repented of the impurity, sexual sin and debauchery in which they have indulged.

Paul did more than put the congregation on the spot; he admitted that <u>he too</u> had some problems in <u>his</u> life. Paul tells them he will be grieved if the congregation hasn't repented of the serious sins in their lives. Unless the congregation's sins were of major importance, why would he fret so much over them? In other words, if "Saved by Grace" is all there is to be concerned about, why did Paul mention the "serious sins"? Weren't they already covered?

2 Peter 3

⁹The Lord is not slow in keeping his promise, as some understand slowness. He is patient with you, not wanting anyone to perish, but everyone to come to repentance.

Peter gives us some comforting news—especially for those who believe in predestination of the most serious order. Jesus doesn't want <u>anyone</u> to perish—he wants everyone to repent and believe in him.

The Book of Revelation provides us with Jesus' final words about repentance. Unlike the comforting, nurturing shepherd we hear in the Gospels, the Jesus of Revelation wants to get our attention before it's too late. Anyone who can read the following passages and not hear the wake-up call is beyond anyone's help, save God alone.

Revelation 2

⁵ "Remember the height from which you have fallen! Repent and do the things you did at first. If you do not repent, I will come to you and remove your lampstand from its place."

Revelation 2

²² "So I will cast her on a bed of suffering, and I will make those who commit adultery with her suffer intensely, unless they repent of her ways."

Revelation 3

³ "Remember, therefore, what you have received and heard; obey it, and repent. But if you do not wake up, I will come like a thief, and you will not know at what time I will come to you."

Jesus goes on to remind us in verse 19 that when he rebukes and disciplines us, it's simply because he loves us.

Revelation 3

¹⁹ "Those whom I love I rebuke and discipline. So be earnest, and repent."

Keep in mind that Jesus' final words in Revelation contain his most important instructions for those who claim him as Savior. If you loved someone and knew that your last advice to them would have a major impact on their eternity, wouldn't those words reflect what was most important?

2

False Teachings

✦

It might look like a duck

The word "truth" is tossed around frequently among those in the religion business. Who has the truth? I won't tell you I have the full truth, but what I do have is plenty of Scriptural references that support what I believe. I don't know of any single pastor or preacher that has <u>all</u> the truth <u>all</u> the time. I don't expect to ever find a man who does possess all of the truth, simply because our human nature prevents that from happening. It's incumbent on the believer to seek out the truth, since each of us is responsible for his own eternity. There are plenty of charismatic preachers out there that have wonderful personalities, but beware—that doesn't mean they're men of honesty.

It's not uncommon for factions in Christianity to point an accusing finger towards another ministry or sometimes specifically towards a pastor or evangelist. Sometimes the accusations are appropriate, sometimes not, but more often than not, the Christian public ends up in a confusing "he said, she said" situation in which they feel compelled to take sides. The Holy Scripture tells us that teachers will be held more accountable than others simply because they can radically shape the eternity of the hearer, and for that reason I will always be open to questions and critique. I've had a variety of ministries for about 7 years now, including email, radio and internet programs, and have received quite a few questions and concerns from the readers and listeners regarding my work. Almost invariably I'll get a message from someone saying they disagree, which is fine, but they seldom offer any Scriptural basis for their position. What they have, in essence, is an opinion, and no one ever got to Heaven on an opinion.

Colossians 2
**⁶So then, just as you received Christ Jesus as Lord, continue to live in him,
⁷rooted and built up in him, strengthened in the faith as you were taught,
and overflowing with thankfulness.**
**⁸See to it that no one takes you captive through hollow and deceptive philosophy, which depends on human tradition and the basic principles of this
world rather than on Christ.**

Paul is alerting the hearers that they need to keep only one thing in mind—the
teachings of Jesus Christ. **"Hollow and deceptive philosophy"** is running rampant in our society, and sadly, most people can be easily deceived with such nonsense. I'm particularly concerned as I write this in 2004 about **"human tradition
and the basic principles of this world"**. We're presently at war in Iraq, and it
seems the American people have largely rejected the words of Jesus Christ calling
for peace and love and traded them for a "get even" mentality. We seem to get
into the mindset that we must protect ourselves even if it means being <u>offensive</u>
rather than simply <u>defending</u> ourselves. I can't even begin to recall how many "9-
11, Never Forget" bumper stickers I've seen in the past 2 years. I agree we
shouldn't forget those who died in that terrible attack, but I think we've gone
beyond "Never Forget" and have embraced "Never Forgive", which is entirely
different. Search every word Jesus ever spoke and see if you can find even a trace
of approval of retaliation. It's simply not there. If anyone wants to get creative
and try to turn Matthew 21:12 (Jesus overturning the money-changer's tables)
into some sort of endorsement of aggression, I'll just have to shake my head and
say, "You don't have much to work with there, friend".

2 Peter 2
**²Many will follow their shameful ways and will bring the way of truth into
disrepute. ³In their greed these teachers will exploit you with stories they
have made up. Their condemnation has long been hanging over them, and
their destruction has not been sleeping.**

I suppose greed takes many forms, but the most noticeable form would likely be
financial greed. A common way for any pastor to make a substantial amount of
money in the church is to have a large congregation and/or have a congregation
that contributes heavily. It's certainly not unusual to hear plenty of sermons on
tithing each year, but it <u>is</u> unusual to hear some hard-line preaching on common
sins such as greed, alcohol abuse, premarital sex, etc. Preaching on such topics as

these would tend to drive people away from the church, or at the very least take the "giving" spirit out of them. In some cases greed might simply be about power. Turn on the TV and watch the strutting about of some of the characters in the religion business that invade your living room each week. In many cases this is a display of pride of the highest order. Being the center of attention is what they're greedy about, and once they're the center of attention, they get what I routinely call "Rush Limbaugh disease". "RLD" is an affliction in which the preacher gets so much adoration from the audience that he actually <u>begins to believe</u> he's always right on every subject he covers. Perhaps "RLD" may need to be renamed "BOD", since Bill O'Reilly seems to have become the national poster boy for "I'm right and everyone else is wrong".

2 Peter 2

[18]For they mouth empty, boastful words and, by appealing to the lustful desires of sinful human nature, they entice people who are just escaping from those who live in error. [19]They promise them freedom, while they themselves are slaves of depravity—for a man is a slave to whatever has mastered him.

Turn on the TV and flip through the television preacher's channels and you'll get a good look at how they can make up doctrine to suit their purposes. The "prosperity" preachers are about the worst in the bunch, but there are certainly plenty of specialty congregations that cater to a wide range of people earnestly trying to find the narrow path to Heaven only to discover that they're <u>still</u> on the wide path, but the preacher has installed attractive curbs to make it look narrow. **"They promise them freedom".**

Jude 1

[4]For certain men whose condemnation was written about long ago have secretly slipped in among you. They are godless men, who change the grace of our God into a license for immorality and deny Jesus Christ our only Sovereign and Lord.

Many internationally known preachers have largely turned the grace of God into a license for immorality. Some of them might mean well, but their constant and unceasing "saved by Grace alone" message has unwittingly placed millions in a trance in which they believe that no real change is needed in their lives as long as they "believe" in Jesus Christ. They sometimes clarify their "grace only" message to say repentance is necessary, but even then they will almost always finish up the message with one more dose of "your sin debt has already been paid—there's nothing you can do on your own to get to Heaven." I agree, there's nothing we can do to get to Heaven, but we can certainly do plenty of things to <u>prevent</u> us from entering paradise.

1 John 3
[7]**Dear children, do not let anyone lead you astray. He who does what is right is righteous, just as he is righteous. [8]He who does what is sinful is of the devil, because the devil has been sinning from the beginning. The reason the Son of God appeared was to destroy the devil's work.**

Among the leading "all grace" preachers in the world is Charles Stanley. May I relate a first-hand account I had in dealing with the Stanley organization? After 9-11, many prominent preachers felt they needed to voice their support for the war in Iraq, and Stanley was no exception. I heard his sermon on the radio and pulled up the transcript from his website. I then contacted his staff and told them he was in error and that I'd provide a point by point rebuttal <u>if</u> they would give him my research. They <u>agreed</u> to do so, and I spent many hours reviewing the Scriptures he used while also seeking Scripture more pertinent to the subject. After sending my research to his associate pastor, I got back a polite email saying something like, "Dr. Stanley is very busy, but he might get an opportunity to look at your work at a later date", followed by a "thank you for your email" type brush-off. I tried unsuccessfully to get in touch with Stanley so I ran his original transcript on my website with my own notes and additional Scripture added. I think this is a simple case of Stanley "not doing right", and then making matters worse by refusing to respond to Scriptural evidence proving he was wrong. It might well be that Stanley has never seen my email nor even heard of it. Many "mega-church" pastors have associate pastors and secretaries who act as a buffer zone between them and the public. One of their chief jobs is to "filter" questions and criticisms leveled at their boss. If they purposely refuse to forward helpful Scriptural information, they're doing evil too.

Ephesians 5
[3]**But among you there must not be even a hint of sexual immorality, or of any kind of impurity, or of greed, because these are improper for God's holy people. [4]Nor should there be obscenity, foolish talk or coarse joking, which are out of place, but rather thanksgiving. [5]For of this you can be sure: No**

immoral, impure or greedy person—such a man is an idolater—has any inheritance in the kingdom of Christ and of God. ⁶Let no one deceive you with empty words, for because of such things God's wrath comes on those who are disobedient.

Noticeably absent from Paul's words here are "saved by grace alone". Among Paul's warnings is a clear declaration: **"For of this you can be sure"**, followed by the various types of people who have no inheritance in Heaven. Paul, as if to use a "one-two punch", further drives the point home in verse 6 by saying, **"Let no one deceive you with empty words, for because of such things God's wrath comes on those who are disobedient"**. Paul, like so many others, puts the responsibility back on the shoulders of the believer.

2 Peter 3
¹⁷Therefore, dear friends, since you already know this, be on your guard so that you may not be carried away by the error of lawless men and fall from your secure position.

I wish I had a nickel for every time I've heard the saying, "We're not under law, we're under grace" and that "a true believer is totally protected by God". I find it interesting that Peter is warning us that **"lawless men"** can have an effect on our **"secure position"**. It certainly sounds like we can be lead astray to a point in which we jeopardize our own Salvation.

Romans 1
²¹For although they knew God, they neither glorified him as God nor gave thanks to him, but their thinking became futile and their foolish hearts were darkened.

How can you "know God" other than to acknowledge him <u>as</u> God? In other words, a person can't say they "know Santa Claus" unless they acknowledge him to be a real person. It seems Paul is saying that although these people admitted God was real, they made an active choice to disregard and disrespect him. Do we?

1 John 2
¹⁹They went out from us, but they did not really belong to us. For if they had belonged to us, they would have remained with us; but their going showed that none of them belonged to us.

My preacher friends love to use this passage to say not all people who profess faith in Christ really <u>have</u> faith in Christ. That's fine, but they remain silent whenever I ask, "Do you guys feel a responsibility in helping these people <u>know</u> that 'they don't belong to Christ?'" I personally believe it's the responsibility of every pastor to advise their congregation on whether the members of his church are true Christians. Yes, I fully understand and agree that only God knows what's in the heart of an individual, but a pastor <u>can</u> certainly talk to a person and learn much about what they think and believe. Once they get a clear profile of that person, they can structure a series of questions to incite that person to either feel confident in their Salvation, or more importantly, give them something to think about to either get them back on the narrow path or help them <u>get on</u> the narrow path. I've told several pastors my suggestion over the years, and I haven't seen one try it yet. Why? "The path of least resistance" will generally prevail in every church.

3

Warnings

◆

*"The wise don't need it,
and fools won't heed it"*

Along with the "Good News", our Bible has many warnings. Jesus Christ himself offers scores of them and his most important Disciples lend their own confirmation. When you read the words of Jesus, just pause for a moment and let them sink in. Don't argue, don't try to reason your way out of them, and most importantly, don't seek protection from any pastor who dismisses your concern as "you worry too much." Pastors like that are on the fast track to Hell with much of their congregation handcuffed to them.

John 12
[47] "As for the person who hears my words but does not keep them, I do not judge him. For I did not come to judge the world, but to save it. [48]There is a judge for the one who rejects me and does not accept my words; that very word which I spoke will condemn him at the last day."

Mark 8
[38] "If anyone is ashamed of me and my words in this adulterous and sinful generation, the Son of Man will be ashamed of him when he comes in his Father's glory with the holy angels."

If we hear the words of Christ, yet don't keep them, what shall we produce for a defense upon our death or the Second Coming? It would seem not keeping the words of Jesus is tantamount to being ashamed of him, and Jesus says very clearly he will be ashamed of anyone who is ashamed of him. I take that to mean Jesus will not admit anyone into his Heaven who is ashamed of him. Isn't that fair? Luke also had some thoughts about those ashamed of Jesus:

Luke 9
²⁶ **"If anyone is ashamed of me and my words, the Son of Man will be ashamed of him when he comes in his glory and in the glory of the Father and of the holy angels."**

How do you define "ashamed"? If a kid doesn't want his father driving him to the prom, that means he doesn't want to be seen publicly in the presence of his father. How many of us "don't want to be seen" with Jesus? Are you willing to talk publicly about your Christian faith? I'm not talking about preaching, necessarily, but I am talking about being faithful enough to let others know you're a Christian. If you find that "unprofessional" or "uncomfortable", you might be flirting with being ashamed of Jesus.

Matthew 10
³⁷ **"Anyone who loves his father or mother more than me is not worthy of me; anyone who loves his son or daughter more than me is not worthy of me; ³⁸and anyone who does not take his cross and follow me is not worthy of me."**

This passage has been preached and taught regularly, yet people will still walk away muttering something about "Jesus doesn't want me to <u>not</u> love my family". They're right, Jesus wants you to love your family <u>and everyone else</u> with a strong love, but what he's saying here is that he wants no competition in our love for <u>him</u>. Our love for Christ should be on a higher plane and unlike any love we feel for family or friends. I don't think we're doing very well in that department, and I certainly don't meet many people who are willing to "take up their cross and follow Jesus", so that tells me the majority of the "professing Christians" out there aren't worthy of Jesus. You figure it out.

Matthew 7
¹⁶ **"By their fruit you will recognize them. Do people pick grapes from thornbushes, or figs from thistles? ¹⁷Likewise every good tree bears good fruit, but a bad tree bears bad fruit. ¹⁸A good tree cannot bear bad fruit, and a bad tree cannot bear good fruit. ¹⁹Every tree that does not bear good fruit**

is cut down and thrown into the fire. ²⁰Thus, by their fruit you will recognize them.
²¹"Not everyone who says to me, 'Lord, Lord,' will enter the kingdom of heaven, but only he who does the will of my Father who is in heaven. ²²Many will say to me on that day, 'Lord, Lord, did we not prophesy in your name, and in your name drive out demons and perform many miracles?' ²³Then I will tell them plainly, 'I never knew you. Away from me, you evildoers!'"

What kind of "fruit" does your tree bear? Are you filled with hatred towards people of other races or nationalities? Are you a lover of war? Do you build with love, or tear down with hate? Ask someone who knows you well to give you a good, honest evaluation. Does a person need to be a religion scholar to understand that a person professing to be a Christian should bear good fruit? Seems real simple to me.

Many Christians are familiar with the passage from Matthew in which Jesus tells the crowd it's better for them to gouge out an eye or cut off a hand that is causing them to sin rather than their entire body being thrown into Hell. I remember very well sitting in a Wednesday night Bible study when this passage came up for discussion. My pastor said, "Clearly, Jesus wasn't serious when he said this, it's simply a parable." Being the analytical person I am, I asked, "How do you figure this is a parable? It doesn't tell a story or make any sort of comparison; rather, Jesus simply says how serious he is about sin." The preacher grunted and grumbled, yet never was able to support his opinion that Jesus was telling a story. Read the passage below for yourself and decide if Jesus is simply talking to hear himself speak, or giving us a stern warning.

Matthew 5
²⁹ "If your right eye causes you to sin, gouge it out and throw it away. It is better for you to lose one part of your body than for your whole body to be thrown into hell. ³⁰And if your right hand causes you to sin, cut it off and throw it away. It is better for you to lose one part of your body than for your whole body to go into hell."

It reads like simple logic to me. "If", this happens, then "do" this. I have something in common with my former pastor, in that I don't take this passage literally either. Does that mean I reject the instruction of Jesus? Not at all, but as the Holy

Spirit continues to clean up my life, I can only imagine I would be blind with no hands due to past sins that burdened me. I think Jesus is trying to tell us, "I'm the better way (in the person of the Holy Spirit) to help with your sin problem, but if you believe in me, yet refuse to utilize the Holy Spirit, you just might need to take some drastic action." For those who think Jesus might have been speaking off-handedly, consider he said the same thing almost word for word 13 chapters later:

Matthew 18
⁸ "If your hand or your foot causes you to sin, cut it off and throw it away. It is better for you to enter life maimed or crippled than to have two hands or two feet and be thrown into eternal fire. ⁹And if your eye causes you to sin, gouge it out and throw it away. It is better for you to enter life with one eye than to have two eyes and be thrown into the fire of hell."

Would Jesus "joke" twice about the same subject? I think not. While we should take <u>all</u> of what Jesus said seriously, there are some parts of his teachings that should really get our full attention. Let's look at some of his instructions from 2000 years ago and see how they might apply today.

Matthew 25
⁴¹ "Then he will say to those on his left, 'Depart from me, you who are cursed, into the eternal fire prepared for the devil and his angels. ⁴²For I was hungry and you gave me nothing to eat, I was thirsty and you gave me nothing to drink, ⁴³I was a stranger and you did not invite me in, I needed clothes and you did not clothe me, I was sick and in prison and you did not look after me.'
⁴⁴ "They also will answer, 'Lord, when did we see you hungry or thirsty or a stranger or needing clothes or sick or in prison, and did not help you?'
⁴⁵ "He will reply, 'I tell you the truth, whatever you did not do for one of the least of these, you did not do for me.'
⁴⁶ "Then they will go away to eternal punishment, but the righteous to eternal life."

Let's begin by listening to what is happening to the people on "his left". **"Depart from me, you who are cursed, into the eternal fire prepared for the devil and his angels."** Can there be any doubt the people he's talking to are bound for Hell? It's important to read and re-read verse 41 until you get a full understanding of what the future is for that group. Now that we're clear on that, let's find out <u>why</u> they're going to Hell. Jesus tells them he was hungry, thirsty, a stranger, needing clothes, and was in prison, but those "on his left" ignored the need. They try in vain to salvage the situation by asking Jesus, "When did we see you in those situations?", to which Jesus responds, **"I tell you the truth, whatever you did not do for one of the least of these, you did not do for me."** It's often been said true Christians operate as the eyes, ears, hands and feet of God while we're on this earth. Can God rectify some of the issues Jesus was concerned about without our help? Absolutely, but we're called to practical Christianity, and practical Christianity <u>always</u> involves action on our part. We have millions of Christians who "worship" God for an hour on Sunday morning, lifting their hands, closing their eyes and "adoring God", yet do we actively seek to share that love with others as we leave the building? Jesus is deadly serious about putting our Christianity into full play, not simply talking about it. You should remember Jesus' warning at the beginning of the passage and now couple it with the last sentence of the passage which says: **"Then they** (those on his left) **will go away to eternal punishment, but the righteous to eternal life."** Does this mean any Christian that fails in any of the categories mentioned will go to Hell? I certainly hope not, since most of us have been negligent in at least one directive, but will my <u>hope</u> overcome the specific <u>instructions</u> of Jesus? I think not, since none of the instructions given are beyond our capabilities. Let's look at them more closely and consider what modern situations exist that parallel what Jesus was referring to. Hunger and thirst—do you know of anyone who is hungry or thirsty? Perhaps we isolate ourselves from those in need by accident, or in some cases, intentionally. In my hometown of Baton Rouge, hungry people aren't as visible as in some other cities. I was in Houston recently and saw a man pulling food out of a dumpster at a fast food restaurant. I probably should have stopped and bought him a meal, but I didn't. I rationalized the situation by telling myself, "John, you can buy the guy a burger tonight, but he'll be right back in the dumpster tomorrow." That's a lame justification of my lack of action, and I'll answer for it one day. What about those who need clothes? Many people can step up proudly and say, "I donate clothes to the Salvation Army every year!" Now please answer honestly: Was it to do a good deed, or did you want that easy tax deduction? This is between you and God, so make it easy on yourself. What about the sick? Oh, sure, we've all been to visit a sick relative or friend, but what about visiting a sick stranger? I have a phobia about being around sick people, so I'd rather not get too involved in that type of ministry. I did, however, have a memorable experience some years ago after being asked to go to the home of a terminally ill man to pray with him.

I knew the man in passing, but I certainly wasn't close to him. Quite frankly, I had never even really prayed with someone in circumstances like that, but I took a shot at it. As I recall, the man was given about a year and a half to live, but he was dead around three months after getting the diagnosis. What did I learn? Among other things, I learned that tough, macho men are probably more afraid to die than anyone else. I learned that people who aren't very spiritual quickly begin to seek out God when they realize they have limited time. And last, but certainly not least, is once a terminally ill person connects to God, and I mean <u>really connect</u>, they begin to get a sense of peace. As I visited the gentleman in question during his final month, I saw the disease take its toll, but I also saw his acceptance of the situation grow. I remember well the last day I saw the man after hospice had set up the final vigil. His wife told me he had been talking out of his head that day, but I saw something very different. As I held his hand he looked me straight in the eyes and said, "I'm ready to go home." He died that afternoon. Although he appreciated my visits, I know I got more from the conversations and prayer sessions than he did, so God blessed me. Although I'm still not overly eager to visit sick people, I do feel much stronger in visiting the terminally ill. I can't quite explain it, but when I'm talking to a person who may only have days or even hours left on this earth, it seems like that's about as close to God as I can get without actually dying myself.

What about visiting people in prison? I took a shot at that too, about 5 years ago. Why did I stop? Honestly, it was too much to bear time-wise. That's a poor excuse, but it's true. We'd meet at the church for 5 PM, drive for about an hour, go into the prison for 3 hours or so, drive back to the church and then I'd have another half hour drive back home. Getting home at 11 PM and getting up the next morning was tough. Once again, I'll have to answer one day for being such a lightweight. One thing I <u>can</u> tell you is that visiting inmates is a special experience. Americans, even American Christians, seem to be very skeptical about inmates who claim a relationship with Jesus Christ. I've heard it called "jailhouse conversion", usually meant as a derogatory reference. Why? Many people believe inmates professing a strong belief in Jesus are simply trying to pull the wool over the public's eyes in order to get out of serving their sentence. I've sat shoulder to shoulder with murderers who have very little hope of ever getting out, but have faith that's much stronger than what you'd find in "freemen". Whether the average Christian ever visits someone in prison is one issue, but being critical and condescending toward those who do visit is inexcusable. During my time of prison ministry, I'd often make this comment to friends, "Boy, those inmates know their Bible a lot better than I do", only to hear this remark, "Well sure, that's all they have to do—sit around and read their Bibles". Sorry, folks, but they can spend their time doing much more than reading their Bible. They can read the Koran, they can read subversive information that will make them better criminals if they ever get released, and, if nothing else, they can spend all of their free time in the exercise yard, making them bigger and stronger to one day overtake a guard or be a greater menace to society if they're released. Please refrain from ever saying or thinking inmates have nothing to do but read their Bibles. Perhaps the reason some Christians are so quick to downplay an inmate's Bible knowledge might be a defense mechanism to prevent the "freemen" from appearing to be Bible ignorant in comparison to the inmate.

Regardless of what you believe about caring for the needs of others as outlined in this passage, you will have a difficult time not understanding the penalty for those who didn't at least make an attempt at satisfying the requirements listed: **"Then they will go away to eternal punishment, but the righteous to eternal life."** Jesus doesn't list any exemptions for those who will, in the future, simply "believe". You're welcome to look at his words from any angle you'd like, but ultimately you must come to accept that Jesus is looking for soldiers in his army, not paper-pushers.

Everyone will generally agree America is a blessed country. I firmly believe being highly blessed by God contributes to the overall feeling that "We're Americans, and we deserve to live well and have plenty of stuff". I've studied people all my life, and I've found that rich people, in most cases, don't have the same hunger for God that a poor person does. Why? It's simple—the poor person has very little materially to get in their way of worshipping God, while the rich person often gets the feeling they're something special, and their belief in God is often less than their belief in <u>themselves</u>. Watch and listen to Donald Trump—can he ever elevate his love of God over his love of himself? God refuses to settle for seconds, folks.

We Americans tend to be very possessive when it comes to our "stuff". I regularly hear people talk about how they "worked hard for everything they've got", and I can identify with that. What needs to be remembered, though, is God blesses many of us with the <u>opportunity</u> to earn money to buy material things. Simply working hard in America is no guarantee of getting ahead. I see fast-food employees who work very hard that may never get ahead in life. Hour for hour, many common laborers work much harder than I do, but most of them will never earn a third of what I earn. I give credit to God for blessing me with any success I have. To even suggest we should be willing to give up everything for Jesus is unfathomable to many Christians, but Jesus spoke very clearly about the subject.

Luke 14
33 "**In the same way, any of you who does not give up everything he has cannot be my disciple.**"

The main reason prospective Christians can't accept this teaching from Jesus is they don't understand what he's saying. Many people assume the worst—that Jesus will make them give up everything they have to be his disciple, and while it's always possible Jesus <u>might indeed</u> ask one to give it all up, let's take a look at another passage that should give us hope:

Matthew 6
31 "**So do not worry, saying, 'What shall we eat?' or 'What shall we drink?' or 'What shall we wear?' 32For the pagans run after all these things, and your heavenly Father knows that you need them. 33But seek first his kingdom and his righteousness, and all these things will be given to you as well.**"

During my 50 years on this earth, I have ignored God, fought God and finally yielded to God. I can say without reservation that yielding to God provides the most serene and peaceful existence possible on this earth. We often lament the complexity of this world, yearning for the "simple life". Jesus is telling us in very direct language if we seek the Kingdom of God and make that our number one priority, God will handle all the rest. I'm still working toward having 100% total faith in God to provide what I need, but what I can say here and now is that with every increase in faith on my part, God answers very quickly and definitively. How can we go to God with a child-like faith that shows God we are ready to follow his instructions? Read on-

Luke 18
17 "**I tell you the truth, anyone who will not receive the kingdom of God like a little child will never enter it.**"

Going to God like a little child is beyond what most adults can comprehend, but as Jesus instructs, that's exactly what we must do. It's very difficult for most of us to be savvy in the ways of the world yet be able to shut off those emotions totally and go to God in prayer to receive his instructions. There were times I went to God in prayer only to be met with silence. Was God ignoring me? Did God misplace my "file", preventing him from considering my questions? Nope, God didn't answer me for one simple reason: He had already provided those answers in Holy Scripture. I believe God expects us to do our own research and study what he said. If we find ourselves in a situation in which we have searched diligently for an answer to a question we have for God, yet come up empty, then God will step in and answer that question specifically for us. Here's a tip that might help some of you: I have often asked God a question and waited and waited for an answer. After a while, I finally gave up and forgot about it. Often, that's precisely when God <u>will</u> answer my question. I can't relate the number of times a thought pops up in my mind that answers some of my deepest questions. When this pattern first started, I thought to myself, "Gee, I can answer my <u>own</u> questions", but then I realized God was answering my questions at a point in time when I grew weary of waiting for his response. Why would God operate like that? I think it's very simple—if we can put God on <u>our</u> timetable, then God works for <u>us</u>. God isn't our buddy or pal, God is God. God, although a loving and nurturing Father, is also the omnipotent, omnipresent God who knows everything that's happened, is happening and will happen. God will never be put in a position to be "our employee". God has <u>his</u> role, and he expects us to honor <u>ours</u> as evidenced in the next passage:

Matthew 12
³⁰ "He who is not with me is against me, and he who does not gather with me scatters."

Although the White House has chosen to take this passage and politicize it, the real meaning is clear and easy to understand, though it's often hard to accept. I think the average Republican Christian has somehow decided that those who aren't "with" Christ are our mortal enemies and must be dealt with. There is nothing Scriptural to support that, rather we serve a Jesus who wants our Christian world to be <u>inclusive</u>, not <u>exclusive</u>. If the true Christians of the world would realize Jesus wants us to clean up our <u>own</u> act in order for us to be a light for the world, life would be much easier. Many Christians simply wander through life without any real passion for seeking Jesus, and for that group Jesus has some stern words:

Revelation 3
[16] "So, because you are lukewarm—neither hot nor cold—I am about to spit you out of my mouth. [17]You say, 'I am rich; I have acquired wealth and do not need a thing.' But you do not realize that you are wretched, pitiful, poor, blind and naked."

I suppose there are many ways this passage can be interpreted, but I tend to believe Jesus is saying, "Get with the program and belong to me, or you're running the very real risk I'm going to reject you". Pray that God will reveal the truth of this passage to you. Many Christians simply fall back on the "I believe in Jesus, so I'm saved" routine that has been perpetrated in the modern church for scores of years. The Apostle Paul is the hero of most Protestants; so let's hear what he has to say on the subject:

1 Corinthians 6
[9]Do you not know that the wicked will not inherit the kingdom of God? Do not be deceived: Neither the sexually immoral nor idolaters nor adulterers nor male prostitutes nor homosexual offenders [10]nor thieves nor the greedy nor drunkards nor slanderers nor swindlers will inherit the kingdom of God. [11]And that is what some of you were. But you were washed, you were sanctified, you were justified in the name of the Lord Jesus Christ and by the Spirit of our God.

Modern teachers frequently dismiss Paul's warning as being only for unbelievers. Do you see anything that says, "Unbelievers will not inherit the kingdom of God"? Heck, that goes without saying. I think Paul's add-on warning of "Do not be deceived" is a good tip that a Christian should read and understand what sort of sinful living might jeopardize their Salvation. Right-wingers love to focus on "homosexual offenders" and throw out the rest of the categories. Let's push the envelope a bit and state that a practicing homosexual claims to be a Christian. Bible-thumpers will say, "They can't be a Christian because they're clearly in violation of 1 Corinthians 6." By the way, I actually heard a caller on a radical Christian talk show cite 1 Corinthians 6 as a condemnation of homosexuals. So, if a homosexual can't be a "real Christian" due to the warnings in 1 Corinthians 6, then we're all in serious trouble. How so? Read the passage and see if you can honestly say you're not guilty of at least one of the other charges. Let's break them down:

Sexually immoral—If you're a young, single person having sex, or even an older person recently widowed having sex outside of the bond of marriage, you're sexually immoral. Slice it and dice it all you want, but that's the facts. I may one day wish I'd never said this, but regardless, it will remain Scripturally true.

Idolaters—Modern Christians seemed to be confused on this one. They seem to think idol worship was limited to people 6000 years ago with Golden Calves and Baal's and Ashtoreths, but an idol can be something as familiar as a Harley Davidson or a Ranger bass boat. How so? If anything in your life becomes a focal point and an object of your constant thoughts, it's an idol. "Oh, but I don't think about my Harley every waking moment." Okay, fair enough, but answer one question honestly—do you think about your Harley more than you think about God? If the answer is yes, your Harley is an idol. I find it sadly funny that the average American Christian wants to fight to keep the 10 Commandments posted everywhere, yet very few can even <u>name</u> all 10 Commandments. What's the first commandment? **"You shall have no other Gods before me"**, and the second? **"You shall not make for yourself idols."** Any other questions on this one? I didn't think so.

Adulterers—Adultery is much more common in our society than many Christians want to admit, and much of it goes on within the Church. It's not unusual to hear about a pastor that begins "counseling" a church member only to end up in bed with her. The rules of adultery extend to a man marrying a woman who didn't have suitable grounds for her divorce. Don't take my word for it, go look it up.

Male prostitutes—While we still have prostitutes, both male and female, I doubt that your average church member falls into this category. If, however, a person sells their body for money and claims to be a Christian, they're only deceiving themselves.

Homosexual offenders—Bisexuals would be included as well, so Madonna should be on alert.

Thieves—Most Christians would read this and simply retort, "Well, I may be many things, but I'm not a thief". Don't be too hasty in making that determination. Do you handle personal business at work while being paid? That's theft. Do you bring home office supplies? Theft. Have you borrowed shop supplies like duct tape or WD40? Theft. What is theft? Quite simply, it's the removal of any tangible item from its rightful owner without having permission. By the way, just because your supervisor said you could take some supplies doesn't let you off the hook. Why? Think about it like this, if the supervisor said it's okay to take something, and the owner of the company came along later and you asked, "Mr. Jones, is it okay for employees to take company property without paying for it?", would Mr. Jones say, "sure, no problem"?

Greedy—Once again, most folks will reject the idea they're greedy. Greedy people have to be like Donald Trump, right? Nope, greedy people are much like you and I—we have more than we need, yet we scratch and claw to get more while there are people all around us barely making ends meet, that is if they're even making them meet at all. I've found one way to try to help those in tough circumstances, and it's called tipping. I'm not a big tipper, but I try to evaluate my server to find out how they're doing in life. We've all seen the waitress that looks like she's about to drop, and she probably has a couple more hours to work before returning home to work another 3 hours or more. We can give a little extra on her tip to help out. Cleaning people in hotels are often forgotten as far as tipping is concerned. Again, I don't leave a wad of cash, but a few dollars from each hotel guest will go a long way. Greed is a sneaky thing—we justify our greed by saying we're saving for our retirement, etc., but if someone is hungry and down on their luck right now, we need to do our best to help the situation.

Drunkards—Who is a drunkard? Again, we have a way of justifying our actions, but if a person gets drunk on a regular basis, I'd have to say they're a drunkard.

Slanderers—Sadly, we find a great many slanderers right in our own churches. Slanderers don't bother to complicate the situation with the facts; they just shoot from the hip. I've been a slanderer, and to some degree, still am one, but with the help of the Holy Spirit, I'll beat that demon.

Swindlers—This is a group that's a little bit harder to nail down. Sure, it's easy to spot the slimy used car salesman who will tell you whatever it takes to sell that clunker, but there are swindlers in our midst that look, act and sound like they're model Christians, while underneath the facade is often the core of a crook. If a person owns a very profitable business yet pays his employees poor wages under the guise of "business is really bad", he's a swindler. If a businessman charges for a particular product, yet ships his customer something inferior to what the customer paid for, he's a swindler.

Now that we've covered all of the categories of people who won't inherit the Kingdom of God, is anyone going to Heaven? Oh, you believe if a person accepts Jesus as their personal Savior, they have an exemption from these "rules"? Okay, then look at category five and tell me what you now think about the homosexual offenders. Can't a homosexual accept Jesus as Savior? Oh, you believe a practicing homosexual is making a choice to sin, so they eliminate themselves from the benefit of Salvation? Better go back and look at the other categories that people routinely practice far more often than homosexuality and think it over. Is there a "sin rating chart" that states a homosexual is worse than a thief? Is a drunk-driver a worse sinner than a homosexual? I think so. Why? It's highly unlikely a homosexual will ever kill me, but the chances are good I might be killed by a drunk-driver.

Ephesians 4
²⁵Therefore each of you must put off falsehood and speak truthfully to his neighbor, for we are all members of one body. ²⁶"In your anger do not sin": Do not let the sun go down while you are still angry, ²⁷and do not give the devil a foothold. ²⁸He who has been stealing must steal no longer, but must work, doing something useful with his own hands, that he may have something to share with those in need.

Although we shouldn't have to be reminded of the teachings above, it would appear most people don't understand we're called to a higher standard as Christians. Let's review them and you can decide for yourself how well you're doing.

Put off falsehood and speak truthfully. A recent survey says most people lie regularly. How much do you lie? Will you ask the Holy Spirit to make you incapable of lying?

In your anger, do not sin. This is a tough one for me, because I tend to get angry quite often. I find it comforting to learn that anger itself isn't a sin, but the action we take while angry can quickly change the situation. There are times anger is a completely legitimate emotion and God understands that, but retaliation and hostility towards those who make us angry isn't allowed. Period.

Steal no longer. Back up a couple of pages and read what Paul said about theft in 1 Corinthians 6.

The Apostle Paul also has a few more things to say about those who <u>won't</u> enter Heaven:

Galatians 5
[19]**The acts of the sinful nature are obvious: sexual immorality, impurity and debauchery;** [20]**idolatry and witchcraft; hatred, discord, jealousy, fits of rage, selfish ambition, dissensions, factions** [21]**and envy; drunkenness, orgies, and the like. I warn you, as I did before, that those who live like this will not inherit the kingdom of God.**
[22]**But the fruit of the Spirit is love, joy, peace, patience, kindness, goodness, faithfulness,** [23]**gentleness and self-control. Against such things there is no law.**

Many pastors will calm down the congregation by saying, "Oh, but Paul is talking about people who haven't accepted Jesus as their Savior. You know that no one's perfect." For those misguided individuals, let's focus on one important sentence in this passage: **"I warn you, as I did before, that those who live like this will not inherit the kingdom of God."** How in the world can anyone take such a clear warning and somehow discount it to mean that we can engage in serious sin and simply dismiss it since we've accepted Jesus as our Savior? It just doesn't work, folks. Paul certainly talks about what will keep us <u>out</u> of Heaven, but he also includes some things that, as followers of Jesus, will assure us passage <u>into</u> Heaven: **"Love, joy, peace, patience, kindness, goodness, faithfulness, gentleness and self-control."** How well is your life characterized by these identifiers?

When I look at modern Christianity and the common beliefs about Christianity, I can imagine that Jesus Christ sits in Heaven and wonders, "How, after all the practical teachings I gave them, can people misunderstand and misapply the fundamentals of being my followers?" Modern Christianity has been reduced to saying some canned lines and showing up at a Promise Keepers rally or buying "The Purpose Driven Life" book. Would it be such a stretch to think Jesus wanted people, while still on this earth, to care for each other and show their devotion to him in practical ways? If Heaven is the payoff, then why would Jesus simply want his people to pay him lip service, yet not do anything practical on this earth? It just doesn't make sense—neither logically nor scripturally. Is it remotely possible

Jesus primarily wants people to just live a holy life and treat people nicely? Let's take a look at some Scripture that discusses this.

John 5

28 "Do not be amazed at this, for a time is coming when all who are in their graves will hear his voice 29and come out—those who have done good will rise to live, and those who have done evil will rise to be condemned."

Jesus seems to speak quite clearly here—**"those who have done good will rise to live, and those who have done evil will rise to be condemned"**. Maybe you think he's only talking about those who never heard the Gospel. What makes you think that?

3 John 1

11Dear friend, do not imitate what is evil but what is good. Anyone who does what is good is from God. Anyone who does what is evil has not seen God.

Long _after_ the resurrection, John records this qualifying statement: **"Anyone who does what is good is from God. Anyone who does what is evil has not seen God."** Is there any reason to believe that persistently evil people can go to Heaven? Read on:

Colossians 3

25Anyone who does wrong will be repaid for his wrong, and there is no favoritism.

Wouldn't you think "no favoritism" _means_ no favoritism? It sounds to me like wrongdoers, regardless of what badge of religious persuasion they wear, will be dealt with for the wrong they've done.

2 Corinthians 5

9So we make it our goal to please him, whether we are at home in the body or away from it. 10For we must all appear before the judgment seat of Christ, that each one may receive what is due him for the things done while in the body, whether good or bad.

There has been and will always be discussions about the various judgments we will face. The passage from Colossians 3:25 simply says that "anyone" who does wrong will be repaid for his wrong, so that sounds pretty inclusive. The passage from 2 Corinthians likewise says **"we must all appear before the judgment seat of Christ"**, so there again; it would certainly seem all of us will receive a judgment. For those who assert that true believers will not be judged, I pose the question, why is "all" and "anyone" mentioned? If the response is "yes, we will be judged, but Christ has already paid the price", then why do we read we will be repaid for our actions? To further expound on the possibilities of this debate, I also question: If life in Heaven is perfect and without any sorrow, then how would punishment have any bearing on the individual <u>after</u> their arrival in Heaven? If Jesus has no plans to punish us for the bad we've done, why would he even go through the exercise?

Galatians 6

[7]Do not be deceived: God cannot be mocked. A man reaps what he sows. [8]The one who sows to please his sinful nature, from that nature will reap destruction; the one who sows to please the Spirit, from the Spirit will reap eternal life.

Every time I read the phrase, "Do not be deceived" I picture Jesus and the Apostles having discussions about what might happen in the future. I can almost hear them agreeing that "some day, people will be deceived by slick preachers that will tell people whatever they want to hear". Sadly, people today are easily deceived, with one easy proof being the routine practice of forwarding emails. I regularly get email asking me to pray for a missing child or to pray for a sick child or any number of other seemingly worthwhile things. Wouldn't it be reasonable to ask some questions before forwarding that same email to dozens of others? I follow up on email like this quite often and have learned in one case, countless people had been forwarded an email requesting prayer for a little boy who was missing. The email listed the phone number of the sheriff's office handling the case. I called the number, and they had received so many calls they had to have a special phone line dedicated to the little boy's case. The recorded message said the boy had already been found alive and well. Want to guess <u>when</u> he'd been found? A year and a half before I called. People are easily misled and deceived on a variety of issues, and Salvation is probably at the top of the list of misunderstood topics. By the way, for you folks that have nothing better to do than forward emails, plug in "internet hoax" in your search engine and you can find out quite easily if you're about to perpetuate false information.

1 John 5
¹⁸**We know that anyone born of God does not continue to sin; the one who was born of God keeps him safe, and the evil one cannot harm him.**

Modern Christian preachers and teachers tell us John didn't mean people simply quit sinning; rather what this passage means is that those who accept Jesus as Savior are <u>excused</u> from their sins, but how can anyone dismiss John's powerful words? "Oh, but you must admit we can't stop sinning altogether—that's impossible." Yes, I fully acknowledge we will never reach a sin-free existence on this earth, but Jesus never, ever gave us a "get out of Hell free card" so we could live however we want. There are specific examples of what Jesus expected, so let's take a look at one:

Luke 13
⁶**Then he told this parable: "A man had a fig tree, planted in his vineyard, and he went to look for fruit on it, but did not find any. ⁷So he said to the man who took care of the vineyard, 'For three years now I've been coming to look for fruit on this fig tree and haven't found any. Cut it down! Why should it use up the soil?'**
⁸ **"'Sir,' the man replied, 'leave it alone for one more year, and I'll dig around it and fertilize it. ⁹If it bears fruit next year, fine! If not, then cut it down.'"**

Did Jesus use the three-year time frame for a reason? I suppose someone can build a case that the three-years has specific relevance, but what I get out it is this: "Time's-a-wastin'", as the old folks used to say. I believe Jesus will never give up on us until there is simply <u>no time left</u>, but I'd say the warning above is for that group of people who habitually "put-off" getting fully engaged in their Christianity. Many people simply use up soil and never produce any fruit. Jesus worked hard and took his responsibilities seriously. There's no reason to think he expects us to live anything but a productive Christian life.

Although the Book of Hebrews was originally attributed to Paul, many modern scholars seem to believe Barnabas or Apollos actually wrote Hebrews. Regardless, what the author has to say cleaves very nicely with the parable Jesus spoke in Luke 13.

Hebrews 6

⁷Land that drinks in the rain often falling on it and that produces a crop useful to those for whom it is farmed receives the blessing of God. ⁸But land that produces thorns and thistles is worthless and is in danger of being cursed. In the end it will be burned.

If we are "the land" and Jesus is "the rain", we must allow him to soak in so we will be productive. I've seen dirt with a high clay content get almost as hard as concrete, and when it rains that type of dirt simply sheds the water rather than absorbing it. Our hearts can be hardened sometimes so severely that even Jesus can't (or won't) penetrate them, but we must do our best to be open and receptive to the Holy Spirit so he can convert us to productive soil, preventing us from being "cursed and burned". The author of Hebrews likes to use fire in other passages as well:

Hebrews 10

²⁶If we deliberately keep on sinning after we have received the knowledge of the truth, no sacrifice for sins is left, ²⁷but only a fearful expectation of judgment and of raging fire that will consume the enemies of God.

When I read this passage from Hebrews, the first word that catches my attention is "deliberately". All of the "grace" people reading this need to understand Jesus doesn't simply look the other way when we engage in <u>deliberate</u> sin. What are some examples of deliberate sin? I could write a book about that, but let's look at some common examples:

A person files a phony claim with their insurance company. This is a premeditated and deliberate act of sin.

A married woman regularly goes out "with the girls" after work to bars. Her friends are all single, and are usually "trolling" for men. The woman knows from past experiences that in the process of hanging out with her single friends she will also be approached by strange men. Ignoring the dangers of simple flirtation, she continues to associate with the single women, with the ultimate conclusion being that she has entered into an adulterous relationship with a man she met in a bar. Knowing fully what <u>could</u> happen, she actively chose to put herself in a situation in which sin ultimately did occur. This is an obvious case of deliberate sin.

For some reason, the debate in the modern church seems to be focused on whether or not all sin is covered by Jesus rather than even remotely suggesting any sort of self-appraisal or self-examination is appropriate to determine whether we're living the life Jesus expects us to live. It seems we're constantly trying to shroud our evil actions rather than aggressively dealing with them. I think one of the greatest lies Christians deal with today is the belief that anyone who is working hard to clean up their life is somehow "working their way to Heaven". This is an insult both to the authentic Christian <u>and</u> to Jesus Christ himself. Relegating Jesus to being nothing more than a cosmic clean-up man for our filthy lifestyles is a <u>true</u> abomination to God. Jesus himself reminds us over and over again that his true servants are actively following him and his "sheep" that refuse to remain in his protective care are taking their eternities in their own hands. Let's see what he says in John 15:

John 15
⁶ "If anyone does not remain in me, he is like a branch that is thrown away and withers; such branches are picked up, thrown into the fire and burned."

How many ways can you define "remain in me"? Can anyone, with a straight-face, say what Jesus means is we can live whatever type of life we want as long as we believe he is the Son of God, arose from the dead, and is able to atone for our sins? I maintain that those who "remain in me" are those who have studied the words of Jesus and make an honest and fervent effort to keep them.

4

Obedience

♦

The foundation of authentic Christianity

Obedience is a theme Jesus and the apostles talked about on a regular basis. Obedience and repentance go hand in hand, and Jesus was very clear about both. Once again, if we simply read the words for what they say and refrain from slanting them to suit our purposes we will gain much.

John 14
15 "If you love me, you will obey what I command."

John 14
21 "Whoever has my commands and obeys them, he is the one who loves me. He who loves me will be loved by my Father, and I too will love him and show myself to him."

John 14
23Jesus replied, "If anyone loves me, he will obey my teaching. My Father will love him, and we will come to him and make our home with him. 24He who does not love me will not obey my teaching. These words you hear are not my own; they belong to the Father who sent me."

"Oh, how I love Jesus" was the main line in a hymn we used to sing regularly in the United Methodist church. Singing the words and practicing the same words are light years apart. In the passages from John 14, Jesus couldn't be any clearer in his teachings about what he expects from us. Notice the word "if" used in John 14 verses 15 and 23. Jesus issues a simple test for us, and sadly, most of us fail it daily. He says, without complicating the issue, if we love him we will obey his commands and teachings. He elaborates in verse 23 by saying <u>if</u> we obey him, **"My Father will love him, and we will come to him and make our home with him."** Isn't that powerful and reassuring? The flipside, of course, isn't very reassuring. **"He who does not love me will not obey my teaching."** Is that hard to fathom? Of course not, but for many of us it <u>is</u> hard to accept. Can anyone who doesn't love Jesus go to Heaven?

Matthew 12
⁵⁰ "For whoever does the will of my Father in heaven is my brother and sister and mother."

I question the common Roman Catholic practice of elevating Jesus' mother Mary to a position too close to that of Jesus. Mary was and is a very special person in the Christian church, but when I read what he said in Matthew 12:50, I'm hearing a clear statement that Jesus is closest to those who <u>do the will of God</u>. So close, in fact, that he considers those who do the will of God to be his brother and sister <u>and</u> mother.

Mark 3
³⁴ "Then he looked at those seated in a circle around him and said, "Here are my mother and my brothers! ³⁵Whoever does God's will is my brother and sister and mother."

Mark related the story in almost the same words, and if you'll keep reading, you'll see Doctor Luke recorded the same teaching as well.

Luke 8
²¹ He replied, "My mother and brothers are those who hear God's word and put it into practice."

John had a little different recollection on the same line of teaching, but rather than calling the obedient ones brother, sister and mother, he said Jesus called them "my disciples". Either way, it's certainly nice to be included in Jesus' inner circle because we take his teaching seriously and try our best to put it into practice.

John 8

³¹To the Jews who had believed him, Jesus said, "If you hold to my teaching, you are really my disciples. ³²Then you will know the truth, and the truth will set you free."

After I began sorting the Scriptures by topic for this book, it became interesting to see who talked the most about the various subjects I cover. The Apostle John probably spent more time than any other Apostle on the topic of obedience. In John's later writings he emphasized the message of obedience with even more fervor. Take a look:

1 John 2

³We know that we have come to know him if we obey his commands. ⁴The man who says, "I know him," but does not do what he commands is a liar, and the truth is not in him. ⁵But if anyone obeys his word, God's love is truly made complete in him. This is how we know we are in him: ⁶Whoever claims to live in him must walk as Jesus did.

I truly appreciate Biblical writings that cut to the chase and leave no room for debate. Listen to the power and authority written by a man many consider to be one of the closest, if not the closest, to Jesus. **"We know that we have come to know him if we obey his commands."** There's that word "if" again, and John gives us a clear hope if we obey Jesus' commands we very likely know Jesus. True, there are some hyper-legalists in the world who can obey everything Jesus commanded and still be lost, but let's not go chasing rabbits at this point. Would you agree the number of these hypothetical observers of the law is a small fraction of those who claim to know Christ, yet have no interest in obeying his commands? If so, let's keep our eye on the prize and continue. **"The man who says, 'I know him,' but does not do what he commands is a liar, and the truth is not in him."** John lays down some mighty tough talk, and I thank God for men like him who didn't pussyfoot around the tough issues. If we surveyed every Christian church in America today and only asked two questions of everyone coming out of the doors, we might be surprised. The questions? (1.) "Do you truly know Jesus?" If the answer is yes, we then ask question (2.) "Do you do what he commands?" I can answer an unequivocal "yes" to the first question, but I'd probably have to stop and think about question two. If I can only give a yes or no answer to #2, the answer would be no. Thanks be to God that he looks at things in far greater depth than man does, so here's my answer for God, not man: "I strive to keep the

commandments of Jesus, but fail regularly. I am, however, aware of the importance and the gravity of his commands, and I regularly pray for God to send the
Holy Spirit to change my mind and actions in order for me to fulfill the commandments of Jesus." Is that good enough? I believe so, but it in no way lets me
off the hook completely. You and I don't <u>need</u> the Holy Spirit to enable us to
dump "friends" who are detrimental to our spiritual health. We don't <u>need</u> the
Holy Spirit to take money out of our pockets to give to shelters that help poor
people or unwed mothers—we already know to do that. I view the Holy Spirit as
a specialist God sends to do jobs we humans are incapable of handling ourselves.
Such as? Such as anger, bitterness, envy, prejudice, negative thoughts, and so on.
Can you see the big difference between what <u>we</u> can do versus the times the Holy
Spirit needs to intervene? I heard a pastor once say: "God has no problem with a
3 month old baby needing his diapers changed, but he certainly has a problem
with a healthy, normal 18 year-old needing his diapers changed." It's all about
growing up and maturing spiritually, yet the church is filled with senior citizens
having little or nothing to show for a "Christian" life of 50 years or more. We
readily accept the fact our employer expects our skills to improve, yet we think we
should be able to lollygag around in our walk with Jesus and still be blessed by
God. Why should we think such things?

It seems like everyone wants to come up with a theological slant regarding "commandments" that will let us off the hook in regards to how we live. Some like to
say that "keeping God's commandments" simply means we accept Jesus Christ as
Savior. Is this true? Partly, but let's dig a bit deeper:

1 John 3
**[23]And this is his command: to believe in the name of his Son, Jesus Christ,
and to love one another as he commanded us. [24]Those who obey his commands live in him, and he in them. And this is how we know that he lives in
us: We know it by the Spirit he gave us.**

The Apostle John states it clearly: Believe in Jesus <u>plus</u> love one another. I've
known hundreds of Christians over the years that have no trouble with the first
part, but fall short on command number two. Loving one another goes beyond
the simplicity and logic of loving those close to us. That's a no-brainer. The challenge to love extends far past that area, though. Since I'm writing this in 2004,
I'll use Osama Bin Laden in this example. Do you love Bin Laden? Most folks
will say no, for understandable reasons. I've known scores of Christians who

think they're only required to love other Christians, but I think the passage above offers no such protection since we're to "love one another". Many Christians will walk away feeling secure that Jesus wouldn't expect them to love someone like Bin Laden who rejects him as Savior. Okay, then how about this for all of you white folks out there: Do you love Jessie Jackson and Al Sharpton? They're American Christians, so there is no exemption for you not to love them, right? By the way, before you start building a case they're not "real" Christians, remember with the measure you use to judge, you too will be judged. That usually gets people's attention.

1 John 5
²This is how we know that we love the children of God: by loving God and carrying out his commands. ³This is love for God: to obey his commands.

I realize my Bible "logic" makes some people uneasy, but unless they can come up with a legitimate way around it, so be it. In the passage above we read: (A.) To love the children of God we must love God and carry out his commands. (B.) If we love God we will obey his commands. Conversely, if we refuse to obey God's commands, we don't love him, right? If we don't love God, is our Salvation still intact?

We often criticize and demean "legalists" in the Bible, but here's an interesting conversation between Jesus and a "teacher of the law". Let's read what they discussed:

Mark 12
²⁸One of the teachers of the law came and heard them debating. Noticing that Jesus had given them a good answer, he asked him, "Of all the commandments, which is the most important?"
²⁹"The most important one," answered Jesus, "is this: 'Hear, O Israel, the Lord our God, the Lord is one. ³⁰Love the Lord your God with all your heart and with all your soul and with all your mind and with all your strength.' ³¹The second is this: 'Love your neighbor as yourself.' There is no commandment greater than these."
³² "Well said, teacher," the man replied. "You are right in saying that God is one and there is no other but him. ³³To love him with all your heart, with all your understanding and with all your strength, and to love your neighbor as yourself is more important than all burnt offerings and sacrifices."

³⁴When Jesus saw that he had answered wisely, he said to him, "You are not far from the kingdom of God." And from then on no one dared ask him any more questions.

I like the last sentence in this passage: **"And from then on no one dared ask him any more questions."** I read that to mean, "This is the essence of worshipping God, and if you do this you can't go wrong." There's another statement Jesus made after the teacher offered his views on the most important commandment that's very revealing, I think. **"You are not far from the kingdom of God"**, says much. We modern Christians want to reduce Christianity to the simple belief that Jesus is the Son of God who died as a substitute for our sins. While this is true, Christians will make no change in this world without putting their faith into practice, and this life is simply a dress rehearsal for the next one.

Luke 18
¹⁸A certain ruler asked him, "Good teacher, what must I do to inherit eternal life?"
¹⁹ "Why do you call me good?" Jesus answered. "No one is good—except God alone. ²⁰You know the commandments: 'Do not commit adultery, do not murder, do not steal, do not give false testimony, honor your father and mother.'"
²¹ "All these I have kept since I was a boy," he said.
²²When Jesus heard this, he said to him, "You still lack one thing. Sell everything you have and give to the poor, and you will have treasure in heaven. Then come, follow me."

The "certain ruler" asked Jesus a very simple, yet profound question: **"What must I do to inherit eternal life?"** How often do we ask this question? I'm 50 years old, have been in church most of my life, have taught Sunday School and Bible study classes, have preached many times, have said the right things, have prayed the right things, but I still find myself in precisely the same situation as the "ruler". Some of you will be puzzled or will feel sorry for me and think, "Poor John, he just hasn't understood Jesus' message of Salvation". Please don't feel sorry for me, rather, feel sorry for the billions of people who've misunderstood the message, yet think they have a full grip on the meaning. Feel even sorrier for the billions of deceased people who mistakenly thought they understood the message and because of their error now reside in Hell. Think about the passage above and place yourself in the position of the ruler. Jesus could have easily said, "Lis-

ten, in the coming months you'll see me get arrested and I'll ultimately be crucified. Don't worry, because I'll be resurrected and that will prove who I am. So all
you have to do is just believe in what I'm telling you and believe I can take your
sins away. That's all you have to do." Did Jesus say anything remotely like that?
Nope, he spoke specifically to the young man just like he speaks to us today. Jesus
isn't about rule keeping; rather he's all about knocking down the barriers that
prevent us from putting him first and foremost in our lives. When Jesus tells the
man, **"You know the commandments"**, he wasn't suggesting anyone could
totally obey the commandments. I think Jesus used the discussion about the
commandments simply to set the stage for highlighting the man's big hang-up:
his wealth. I see a world of Christians who know how to "play the game". They
know which Christian lingo to use, they know what organizations they need to
join to be a "visible" Christian, but overall, it's still just a game. We can play
those games in the corporate world, but Jesus will have none of this foolishness in
his world. In the ruler's case, it was all about possessions—he didn't want to give
up his "stuff". What is the barrier between you and Jesus? Is it your job? Your
position in society? Is it your family? We tend to believe worshipping family is
something God approves of, but anything or anyone elevated to a point remotely
close to Jesus is idolatry, and Jesus won't go for that.

Romans 2

**⁵But because of your stubbornness and your unrepentant heart, you are stor-
ing up wrath against yourself for the day of God's wrath, when his righteous
judgment will be revealed. ⁶God "will give to each person according to what
he has done." ⁷To those who by persistence in doing good seek glory, honor
and immortality, he will give eternal life. ⁸But for those who are self-seeking
and who reject the truth and follow evil, there will be wrath and anger.
⁹There will be trouble and distress for every human being who does evil: first
for the Jew, then for the Gentile; ¹⁰but glory, honor and peace for everyone
who does good: first for the Jew, then for the Gentile. ¹¹For God does not
show favoritism.**

Some tend to believe modern Christians are exempt from the warnings in Scripture, but who was Paul referring to in the book of Romans? The Church. Who
was he specifically talking to? The stubborn and unrepentant. What will become
of them? They are storing up God's wrath which will be used against them. Can
you step away from easy-believism for just a moment and consider verse 7? **"To
those who by persistence in doing good seek glory, honor and immortality,**

he will give eternal life." Is it so difficult to understand that our <u>natural</u> actions will reveal our ultimate destiny? Some of you will shout "legalism!" and dismiss my views, but consider what Paul is saying. Can an evil person "persist in doing good" to avoid Hell? No, you can't buy a ticket to Heaven. What you can do, if you're a true believer, is verify that your ticket to Heaven is <u>genuine</u> by examining your actions. If you have no concern for the eternity of other people, your ticket may be a fake. Please understand I'm not talking about just caring for your family and friends—I'm talking about caring for your enemies and for those who persecute you. We're told below it's hard for righteous people to be saved, much less the ungodly.

1 Peter 4
[17]For it is time for judgment to begin with the family of God; and if it begins with us, what will the outcome be for those who do not obey the gospel of God? [18]And,
> **"If it is hard for the righteous to be saved,**
>   **what will become of the ungodly and the sinner?"**

John 8
[54]Jesus replied, "If I glorify myself, my glory means nothing. My Father, whom you claim as your God, is the one who glorifies me. [55]Though you do not know him, I know him. If I said I did not, I would be a liar like you, but I do know him and keep his word."

I find it interesting most Christians don't feel they "have" to keep God's word, yet the man they claim as Savior very clearly tells us <u>he</u> keeps God's word. It almost comes across that we relegate Christ to a lower position than we place ourselves. Was Jesus capable of fully keeping God's word? Yes. Are we? No, but the real issue is "how hard do we try?", that is, if we try at all. "But John, we're no longer under law, we're under grace". Keep reading-

2 Thessalonians 1
[8]He will punish those who do not know God and do not obey the gospel of our Lord Jesus.

Many folks like to argue that when Jesus was giving us instructions on how to live, it was prior to his resurrection, therefore we should "keep things in context".

If that's true, how do we explain the instructions Paul gave to the Thessalonian Christian Church long <u>after</u> the resurrection? Knowing God and obeying the Gospel of our Lord are the ways to escape the punishment of God, not simply wearing a cross pin or having a Jesus fish on the bumper of our car. Maybe this is too complicated, so here's a passage that's simple as can be:

James 4
[17]Anyone, then, who knows the good he ought to do and doesn't do it, sins.

I once knew a Southern Baptist pastor who, in an unguarded moment said, "Sometimes I wish the book of James had never been written." Sorry, preacher, but it <u>was</u> written, and many consider James to be the half-brother of Jesus, so James probably knew Jesus better than anyone. James frequently cuts to the chase and makes statements like the one above that make "nominal Christians" or "carnal Christians" uneasy. Read it again and see if there's any way to misunderstand it. **"Anyone, then, who knows the good he ought to do and doesn't do it, sins."** You don't need me to create a list of things specifically for you, but how about a few simple ones to think about? Speeding, drunk driving, playing loud music in your apartment that bothers others, not providing your employer with 8 hours of work for 8 hours of pay, etc. Some folks, like my pastor friend, like to downplay what James said. Okay, let's hear what "The Man" had to say:

Luke 6
[46]"Why do you call me, 'Lord, Lord,' and do not do what I say?"

Jesus knew there would be plenty of people who would claim him as Savior, yet not heed his instructions. When we read the words of James, we simply hear a confirmation of what Jesus already said. James didn't break any new ground, rather he simply reminds us of the instructions we've <u>already received</u>.

James 1
[22]Do not merely listen to the word, and so deceive yourselves. Do what it says.

I think it's important to realize if we hear the teachings of Jesus and ignore them, we are indeed deceiving ourselves. "But John, we aren't capable of totally keeping the commandments!" True, but once again, the real question is, "how hard are we trying?"

John 8
51 "I tell you the truth, if anyone keeps my word, he will never see death."

Two people read the passage above. One says, "Jesus just means we have to believe in him", while the other says, "Jesus is expecting us to keep his word, meaning we have to follow his instructions." If you read this passage a thousand times, doesn't it appear to be saying the latter?

1 John 2
17The world and its desires pass away, but the man who does the will of God lives forever.

As time passed, the great Apostle John's writings leaned more toward active Christianity. I think it's important to consider that John's writings in the Gospels were much like what Matthew, Mark and Luke wrote, but in 1 John, 2 John and 3 John he shifts gears and focuses on how the believer should live. If one reads the Gospel of John, then reads 1,2 and 3 John, he will see John reiterating what Jesus taught before he was taken up to Heaven. At the risk of overemphasizing the situation, consider the book of Mark was written somewhere around AD 60, and that 1, 2 and 3 John could have been written as late as AD 95. With that thought in mind, the passage above was written around 95 years <u>after</u> the death of Jesus. By this time, the resurrection of Jesus would be an old story, right? If we're in agreement with this concept, why wouldn't John have said, "The world and its desires pass away, but the man who <u>believes Jesus can take away his sins</u> lives forever"? I think it's of extreme importance John specifically talks about doing the will of God. What is the will of God? Most Christians might say, "How about the Ten Commandments?" It's tragically funny the average American Christian is ready to fight to keep the Ten Commandments posted in Judge Roy Moore's courtroom in Alabama, yet how many could recite the Ten Commandments if someone held a gun to their head? This is classic Christian hypocrisy—demand God's word be publicly displayed; yet not even know what God said. Much talk, no walk. Heavy cloud, no rain.

Philippians 2
8And being found in appearance as a man,
    he humbled himself
    and became obedient to death—
        even death on a cross!

Jesus was a man who was obedient to his Father's will, "even death on a cross". Jesus took the bullet for us, so what do we owe him? Quite frankly, everything. If I could have had a conversation with Jesus prior to the crucifixion, it might have gone something like this: (Jesus) "John, I'm going to allow myself to be crucified on a cross so that your sins will be covered. There will be no more blood sacrifices, no ritualistic cleansing. All I ask is that you follow my instructions the best you can." (John) "Jesus, I'll try hard to adhere to your teachings, but I'm weak, so I don't know if I can keep them totally." (Jesus) "John, I'm dying on that cross so you can get away from the law—I am the law. I know no one can keep my word completely, but you must do your best and not simply take the attitude you can live any way you desire. Do we have an agreement?"

What would you say if you had been able to have this conversation with Jesus? I'd say most people would readily take Jesus up on his offer, but unfortunately, not too many of us seem to want to follow through on our part of the bargain.

Hebrews 5
⁷During the days of Jesus' life on earth, he offered up prayers and petitions with loud cries and tears to the one who could save him from death, and he was heard because of his reverent submission. ⁸Although he was a son, he learned obedience from what he suffered ⁹and, once made perfect, he became the source of eternal salvation for all who obey him ¹⁰and was designated by God to be high priest in the order of Melchizedek.

Jesus learned obedience from what he suffered, but do we? I recall having a conversation with a very nice Atheist a few years ago, and he related the following story: He had been a Christian for about 20 years when his young daughter became seriously ill. The little girl ultimately died, and the man decided a loving God wouldn't have taken his daughter. He ultimately turned his back on God and became a practicing Atheist. I don't know how I would feel if I lost a young child, but things happen in this life we often don't understand. To sit back and reap all of the benefits of Christianity yet bail out on the first bit of adversity is one-sided and selfish. Could anything be worse than losing a precious, innocent little girl? What if that little girl grew up into a rebellious teenager who became addicted to a lifestyle of drugs and illicit sex? What if she ultimately became a common prostitute, selling her body for another hit of cocaine? If a father was faced with the choice of losing an innocent little girl to Heaven, or losing a rebellious unbelieving adult daughter to Hell, which would a <u>good</u> father choose? The point is simple—God knows all and sees all, whereas our vision is very limited in scope.

5

Treatment of Others

✦

The practical side of Salvation

In our American perspective, the treatment of others is often overlooked or at least minimized. We seem to be a nation of extremes: on the one hand we frequently don't care what happens to others, yet at other times we show a huge outpouring of concern. As I'm proof-reading this book in early 2005, more evidence emerges to support this theory. The newspaper recently reported a "stray" bomb destroyed a house in Iraq, killing 14 family members and injuring others. At the same time, the United States is rushing aid to the victims of the killer Tsunami that devastated Indonesia. Also in the newspaper today is a story featuring Colin Powell's trip to Africa. Powell is in the country to promote AIDS awareness, yet the genocide in Darfur continues. If the United States is as concerned about human rights in Iraq as we're told, what are we doing to support human rights in Darfur? And so, if we aren't a nation of extremes, we must at least acknowledge we are a nation of conflicting actions. Some might argue when you balance out the two extremes, a healthy condition emerges. Unfortunately, that's not the case, and I'll explain why. I'll use an example we've all seen before. The six o'clock news features a story in which a local family, living in the "bad section" of town, is a victim of a burglary. It's almost Christmas, and all of the gifts for the young children have been stolen. Before it's all said and done, thousands of dollars and hundreds of gifts have been sent to the family. On the one hand, that's wonderful, but on the other hand, it simply shows the imbalance that exists on a daily basis. You can be sure another family in that same town has had a similar fate, but the news people can't "wear-out" the heart strings-tugging story topic. You can also be sure that hundreds of local families living in poverty never had the money to buy gifts in the <u>first place</u>, but that seldom gets discussed either. It's almost comical, in a tragic way—the American public will often race to "rescue" a poor family in financial trouble at Christmas, yet if the Federal Government starts talking about raising the minimum wage, compassion is quickly overtaken by Bubba's concern that the price of a #3 Value Meal will increase by nine cents. Go figure.

John 13
[34] "A new command I give you: Love one another. As I have loved you, so you must love one another. [35]By this all men will know that you are my disciples, if you love one another."

How do we love one another? The average Christian loves his family, his friends, and maybe a few people in his church. Other than that, we seldom extend love to strangers in any tangible way. Notice in the passage above that Jesus doesn't say, "A new <u>suggestion</u> I give you". Jesus lets us know up front he's issuing a <u>commandment</u>. How can we find out positively what Jesus has in mind in regards to loving others? It's really pretty simple: God gave us the Holy Spirit to serve as an earthly intermediary after Jesus rejoined God in Heaven. We can simply ask God to send the Holy Spirit to us individually and he can and will illuminate our minds with whatever God wants us to know. It sounds simple, it <u>is</u> simple, and best of all, it works.

Galatians 5
[13]You, my brothers, were called to be free. But do not use your freedom to indulge the sinful nature; rather, serve one another in love. [14]The entire law is summed up in a single command: "Love your neighbor as yourself." [15]If you keep on biting and devouring each other, watch out or you will be destroyed by each other.

Christians often allow their freedom to imprison them all over again. For those who cling to the "once saved, always saved" lifeboat, it's no big deal, but for those like me who believe Salvation can indeed be forfeited, our freedom is tentative at best. How any Christian can condense the teachings and commandments of Jesus to mean "all you have to do is love Jesus" is beyond me. Jesus doesn't need Christians to sit around worshipping him with lip service; rather he wants us to be his hands, eyes, ears and feet on this earth. He wants us to intervene in every situation in which <u>he</u> would intervene. I'm always impressed with Christians who go into the housing projects to witness for Christ. They're often putting themselves in great physical danger, or at the very least subject themselves to ridicule and taunting. Their actions show true Christian love for their neighbor.

1 Peter 1
²²Now that you have purified yourselves by obeying the truth so that you have sincere love for your brothers, love one another deeply, from the heart.

Peter reveals an important concept here that many Christians blow past: Christians can purify themselves by obeying Jesus. Does this mean we can <u>save</u> ourselves? Of course not, but it <u>does</u> indicate we have a role in our individual purification.

1 John 4
⁷Dear friends, let us love one another, for love comes from God. Everyone who loves has been born of God and knows God. ⁸Whoever does not love does not know God, because God is love.

I know many well-meaning Christians who firmly believe it's acceptable to hate people different than themselves. They'd probably say, "I don't hate them, I just don't like them". Okay—in the passage above, we're <u>not</u> instructed <u>not</u> to hate anyone, we're instructed to <u>love one another</u>. **"Whoever does not love does not know God"** is a pretty strong statement. How's your love for other people these days? Don't try to cop-out by thinking about friends, family and coworkers—think about the worst of the worse. How much do you love Bin Laden? How about Islamic extremists? How about Muslims in general—even the peace-loving kind? Loving the lovable is easy, but loving the unlovable only comes from God. Having trouble loving your enemies? That's not uncommon, but here's the real question: Have you <u>asked</u> God to change your heart and mind, empowering you to love everyone? As humans, we're programmed to <u>not</u> love, and although that's something we may not have any control over, if you refuse to ask God to intervene, you've taken on the entire burden of that sin.

1 John 2
⁹Anyone who claims to be in the light but hates his brother is still in the darkness.

I think this is interesting: **"who claims"** certainly covers the bulk of the modern church. There are people all around us who claim much, but their deeds prove otherwise. You don't hate anyone? Don't be so sure. If you're white and you have a teenage daughter, will you be happy if she shows up with a black boyfriend? Maybe you're a staunch Southern Baptist and your son just announced his fiancé is a Hindu. How does that make you feel? For years I attended an all-white Methodist church, and upon asking why we didn't have any black people in our congregation, and elderly lady said, "They've got their church and we've got ours. We don't bother each other." That was an interesting way to state we were a church of bigots. I don't go there anymore.

1 John 3

[14]We know that we have passed from death to life, because we love our brothers. Anyone who does not love remains in death. [15]Anyone who hates his brother is a murderer, and you know that no murderer has eternal life in him.

Hate is an emotion many of us feel, yet we reject the idea we're capable of hating. I see hatred rear its ugly head on a regular basis, and I know it's very much a part of our society. Some folks will read the passage above and say, "The writer is saying we must not hate a brother in Christ." Frankly, I think that's a narrow interpretation, but for the moment, I'll play along. Let's assume, for a moment, that John is specifically referring to a brother in Christ. If you happen to be a racist, do you immediately exhibit love for a person of another color….if he or she is a Christian? I've been around racists all my life, and I've never heard one, upon being displeased with a person of a different skin color, shout a racial epithet after asking the offender if they're a Christian. It has been said that Sunday morning is the most segregated time slot in America. We quietly go to our mostly segregated churches with thoughts like the lady I mentioned earlier. If you don't recall her words, they go something like this, "We don't bother them, and they don't bother us." I can't help but think God is watching our actions very closely on Sunday morning, and I'm guessing his master plan goes something like this: "If you don't want to worship on earth with those different than you, why should I think you'll want to spend eternity with them, shoulder to shoulder?"

1 John 4

[12]No one has ever seen God; but if we love one another, God lives in us and his love is made complete in us.

The tiny word "if" seems to be a consistent part of Scriptural conditions for Salvation. **"If we love one another, God lives in us"** certainly indicates that if logic prevails, anyone who <u>doesn't</u> love other people <u>doesn't</u> have God living in them. Some lukewarm Christians will protest: "Jesus died for all of my sins, and that happens to be one of my sins." Okay, I'll agree Jesus died for our sins, but unless you honestly and fervently ask God to change your feelings about other people, you've just become the eternal owner of that sin—lock, stock and barrel.

1 John 4
[21]And he has given us this command: Whoever loves God must also love his brother.

John has much to say about love, and his words leave very little "wiggle room". **"Whoever loves God must also love his brother"** is a strong directive. Is there any possible way to get around it? I can't see any.

Matthew 18
[32] "Then the master called the servant in. 'You wicked servant,' he said, 'I canceled all that debt of yours because you begged me to. [33]Shouldn't you have had mercy on your fellow servant just as I had on you?' [34]In anger his master turned him over to the jailers to be tortured, until he should pay back all he owed.
[35] "This is how my heavenly Father will treat each of you unless you forgive your brother from your heart."

Jesus tells this story to fully illustrate how God's very simple plan of Salvation is supposed to work. God, in his infinite mercy, forgives us, but.........very fairly asks us to forgive each other as well. Just to be sure no one tries to get too creative on interpreting this passage, take a look at what Jesus said earlier in Matthew:

Matthew 6
[14] "For if you forgive men when they sin against you, your heavenly Father will also forgive you. [15]But if you do not forgive men their sins, your Father will not forgive your sins."

I've heard people say, "I'll forgive, but I won't forget". When I hear this, I automatically think, "Forgiving is a difficult process, but the most critical step in forgiving is allowing ourselves to <u>forget</u> some of the treatment we've suffered."

When I see the "9-11….Never Forget" bumper stickers, I almost cringe. I don't know what the writer had in mind when he or she penned that famous slogan, but if it means anything other than "Let's never forget about the people we lost on that horrific day", we're flirting with disaster. Notice in the passage above Jesus didn't give us the option of restricting our forgiveness to fellow Christians. He simply says "men", which would indicate he expects us to forgive all men—even terrorists. Is this a tough assignment? Absolutely, but aren't most "born again" Christians always talking about the incredible power of Jesus Christ? Here's where the rubber meets the road—if these "Super Christians" really believe Jesus Christ can do anything, then they <u>must</u> believe Jesus can change their hearts, too. Jesus can change anyone's heart, but before he can, <u>we must ask him to</u>. The Apostle Paul may be an unusual case in which Jesus changed someone who didn't ask, but how would any of us know for sure whether Saul offered a prayer up to God seeking answers to his questions about the validity of Christ?

Matthew 7

[1] **"Do not judge, or you too will be judged. [2]For in the same way you judge others, you will be judged, and with the measure you use, it will be measured to you."**

If every Christian studied only one instructional passage with any diligence, this might be the one to choose. The payback for our judgmental attitudes is heavy. Since I'm a judgmental person, this Scriptural warning frightens me.

Luke 6

[37] **"Do not judge, and you will not be judged. Do not condemn, and you will not be condemned. Forgive, and you will be forgiven."**

Luke simply restates what Matthew said. By the way, there is a big difference between judging someone and making an observation. Example: If I say, "I'll bet Jim uses drugs", I'm judging him. If I see Jim snorting cocaine and say, "Jim uses drugs", I've simply made an observation with no judgment attached. Can you see the difference?

Romans 12

[9]**Love must be sincere. Hate what is evil; cling to what is good. [10]Be devoted to one another in brotherly love. Honor one another above yourselves.**

¹¹Never be lacking in zeal, but keep your spiritual fervor, serving the Lord. ¹²Be joyful in hope, patient in affliction, faithful in prayer. ¹³Share with God's people who are in need. Practice hospitality.

¹⁴Bless those who persecute you; bless and do not curse. ¹⁵Rejoice with those who rejoice; mourn with those who mourn. ¹⁶Live in harmony with one another. Do not be proud, but be willing to associate with people of low position. Do not be conceited.

¹⁷Do not repay anyone evil for evil. Be careful to do what is right in the eyes of everybody. ¹⁸If it is possible, as far as it depends on you, live at peace with everyone. ¹⁹Do not take revenge, my friends, but leave room for God's wrath, for it is written: "It is mine to avenge; I will repay," says the Lord. ²⁰On the contrary:

"If your enemy is hungry, feed him;

   if he is thirsty, give him something to drink.

In doing this, you will heap burning coals on his head." ²¹Do not be overcome by evil, but overcome evil with good.

Paul, the "Grace man" gives us good instructions in Romans 12. How well could the average Christian do if this was a questionnaire? While Paul doesn't list any of the conditions above to be necessary for Salvation, it is of great importance he takes the time to list them. When I read the part about "Do not take revenge", I think about capital punishment. Call me a bleeding-heart liberal if you must, but I fear that executing criminals is taking revenge, and as you can read in the passage above, God says, **"It is mine to avenge; I will repay."**

Luke 6

³⁵ "But love your enemies, do good to them, and lend to them without expecting to get anything back. Then your reward will be great, and you will be sons of the Most High, because he is kind to the ungrateful and wicked. ³⁶Be merciful, just as your Father is merciful."

Again, no specific connection to Salvation, but a wonderful lesson for those who want to follow Christ. It is crucial, however, to note Luke does mention a "great reward" for those who follow these instructions. What might that great reward be? Heaven, perhaps?

Galatians 5
⁶For in Christ Jesus neither circumcision nor uncircumcision has any value. The only thing that counts is faith expressing itself through love.

Paul makes a comment here that certainly indicates action on the part of the believer is critical. **"The only thing that counts is faith expressing itself through love."** We can talk and talk about our faith, but if our faith can't be expressed through love, what kind of faith is it? What value would it have? "Lord, Lord"?

Hebrews 12
¹⁴Make every effort to live in peace with all men and to be holy; without holiness no one will see the Lord.

How will we see the Lord? By muttering empty words? No. By talking about what a great man Jesus was? No. How then? <u>By living a holy life</u>—that's what pleases Jesus. Not "fake" holiness that relies on the work of man, but rather a holiness that only comes from following Jesus Christ and his teachings. How people can claim to love Jesus, yet reject his instructions, is a mystery to me.

We can all agree Jesus talked much about love of fellow man, but he also talked about the <u>absence</u> of love.

Matthew 26
⁵² "Put your sword back in its place," Jesus said to him, "for all who draw the sword will die by the sword."

The average Christian thinks Jesus is leading us in every war we take on, but I don't see any evidence of that. How do we know if Jesus supports a particular war? Do we win that war? If so, was Jesus against Vietnam since we were defeated? I think Jesus speaks quite clearly on this subject in Matthew 26. It simply stands to reason that those of us who live by the sword, or M16, or Patriot Missile might someday die by one or more of these devices. Am I a pacifist? Not really, but I do see a big difference between defending myself versus taking an offensive position "just in case" someone might be thinking about hurting me.

Acts 4

[34]There were no needy persons among them. For from time to time those who owned lands or houses sold them, brought the money from the sales [35]and put it at the apostles' feet, and it was distributed to anyone as he had need.

Where did we go wrong? The early apostles treated each day like it could be their last, pooling their money and looking out for each other. I'm not a history buff, but I understand the early settlers in America also took care of each other. When did that end? It appears that the Welfare program in the U.S. apparently became the accepted method for looking out for our brothers and sisters. Is that what Jesus had in mind? I think not.

6

What did Jesus say?

✦

When all else fails, listen to the Good Shepherd

Why would I push a chapter entitled "Jesus Said" this far back in my book? We've already heard the words of Jesus in the preceding five chapters, but now we hear <u>only</u> from Jesus. My reason for this chapter placement is simple—I've lead you up to this point with interwoven testimony from Jesus and his Apostles. In doing so, I feel I'm building a case for "active Christianity". Chapter 6 is the literary equivalent of the "one-two punch", and by the time the reader finishes this chapter, the true path to Salvation should be clear, that is if the words of Jesus have any merit.

Matthew 19
[16]**Now a man came up to Jesus and asked, "Teacher, what good thing must I do to get eternal life?"**
[17] **"Why do you ask me about what is good?" Jesus replied. "There is only One who is good. If you want to enter life, obey the commandments."**
[18] **"Which ones?" the man inquired.**
[19]**Jesus replied, "'Do not murder, do not commit adultery, do not steal, do not give false testimony, honor your father and mother,' and 'love your neighbor as yourself.'"**
[20] **"All these I have kept," the young man said. "What do I still lack?"**
[21]**Jesus answered, "If you want to be perfect, go, sell your possessions and give to the poor, and you will have treasure in heaven. Then come, follow me."**
[22]**When the young man heard this, he went away sad, because he had great wealth.**

I've always found this story to be very important. By the time Matthew recorded this incident in his Gospel account, Jesus had been among the people extensively. Jesus could have easily answered, "Believe that I am the Messiah and you will have eternal life", but he didn't. Jesus specifically reminded the man of certain commandments, including four from the Ten Commandments and the final commandment as one Jesus issued during his earthly ministry. Jesus, being God, knew exactly what was in the man's heart. He knew the man observed the law, yet still clung to his wealth and possessions. Jesus knew the content of that man's heart, just like he knows the content of our hearts. What are you and I clinging to that might prevent us from having "treasure in heaven"? Isn't it time to remove that stumbling block?

Mark 10

17As Jesus started on his way, a man ran up to him and fell on his knees before him. "Good teacher," he asked, "what must I do to inherit eternal life?"
18 "Why do you call me good?" Jesus answered. "No one is good—except God alone. 19You know the commandments: 'Do not murder, do not commit adultery, do not steal, do not give false testimony, do not defraud, honor your father and mother.'"
20""Teacher," he declared, "all these I have kept since I was a boy."
21Jesus looked at him and loved him. "One thing you lack," he said. "Go, sell everything you have and give to the poor, and you will have treasure in heaven. Then come, follow me."
22At this the man's face fell. He went away sad, because he had great wealth.
23Jesus looked around and said to his disciples, "How hard it is for the rich to enter the kingdom of God!"

Mark's version of this story adds: **"Jesus looked at him and loved him"**. I love that line. Jesus, as God in the flesh, had the ability to look into the man's heart. What did Jesus see? He saw the same thing he would see in many of us: A sincere desire to one day be a citizen of Heaven, yet earthly possessions and hang-ups were preventing that from happening. By the way, many of us will read this story and decide, "I'm not rich, so the story doesn't apply to me." Perhaps you should consider what the meaning of rich is. I believe riches begin as soon as our basic needs are met.

Matthew 16
²⁴**Then Jesus said to his disciples, "If anyone would come after me, he must deny himself and take up his cross and follow me. ²⁵For whoever wants to save his life will lose it, but whoever loses his life for me will find it."**

It's interesting that Jesus didn't say, "If anyone would come after me, I'd <u>prefer</u> he deny himself…" No, Jesus said, **"He <u>must</u> deny himself…"** How does this direct quote from Jesus mesh with the common notion, "All you gotta do is just believe in Jesus"? Why don't you read the entire passage a few times just to let it sink in? Jimmy Swaggart places great importance on the Cross of Christ, but Jesus' emphasis here is on taking up <u>our</u> cross.

Mark 8
³⁴**Then he called the crowd to him along with his disciples and said: "If anyone would come after me, he must deny himself and take up his cross and follow me."**

How can anyone read these words of Jesus and think, "Jesus says all I have to do is believe he can take away my sins and I'm Heaven-bound"? Read it again: **"If anyone would come after me, he must deny himself and take up his cross and follow me."** "He must deny himself", "take up his cross and follow me". Must is a strong word. Jesus could have said, "should", "could", "might", or any other variant of words that suggest he's giving a <u>choice</u> to those who will follow him. Jesus very clearly states we must deny ourselves, take up our cross and follow him. For those of you so brain-washed as to not understand this, please read everything Jesus said in the Gospels very closely. After you do that, if you can still cling to your "just believe" mentality, there is nothing I can do except pray for you. I don't say that in a flippant way, rather I offer it in total sadness that the world is being lead astray with easy believism.

John 8
¹²**When Jesus spoke again to the people, he said, "I am the light of the world. Whoever follows me will never walk in darkness, but will have the light of life."**

Do we hear, "Whoever believes in me"? Nope, Jesus says: **"whoever <u>follows</u> me."** Big difference.

Luke 13
²³Someone asked him, "Lord, are only a few people going to be saved?"
²⁴He said to them, "Make every effort to enter through the narrow door, because many, I tell you, will try to enter and will not be able to."

Who is Jesus talking about? Is it "the lost"? I don't think so, since the lost generally don't acknowledge any Heaven or Hell anyway. The lost, unlike some other folks, don't pretend to be in line for any blessings. So who is Jesus talking about? I think he's talking about the majority of the church. Some folks think the "narrow door" is Jesus, but I think the narrow door <u>leads to Jesus</u>. The narrow door represents a disciplined life dedicated to the Lord Jesus Christ. **"Make every effort"** certainly suggests that Jesus thinks we have the ability to pursue the life he wants us to lead.

John 8
¹⁰Jesus straightened up and asked her, "Woman, where are they? Has no one condemned you?"
¹¹ "No one, sir," she said.
"Then neither do I condemn you," Jesus declared. "Go now and leave your life of sin."

The story of Jesus talking to the adulteress is one of my favorites. The easy-believists in the church will simply say, "Jesus accepts us just as we are", but studying the passage above for a few more moments reveals that although Jesus accepted her as she was, <u>he expected her to change</u>. **"Go now and leave your life of sin"** is a directive for the woman, and us, to clean up our act. Can any one of us honestly say, "I don't commit a single sin I couldn't stop committing on my own"?

John 15
⁴ "Remain in me, and I will remain in you. No branch can bear fruit by itself; it must remain in the vine. Neither can you bear fruit unless you remain in me."

Jesus makes a very simple offer to us: **"Remain in me, and I will remain in you."** Is that hard to comprehend? How do we remain in Christ? By paying him lip service? Does anyone out there really think Jesus will accept an "I believe in you" when the person making that statement lives a life of calculated disobedience? Like what? How about the "Christian" who is planning an abortion? If that woman is saying, "Lord, I believe in you" while having a living person inside her executed, what are those words worth? If a Christian woman reading this has had an abortion and was ignorant of the implications due to poor guidance from her church, I ask you to please go to God in repentance and prayer. Don't automatically assume you're forgiven if you don't understand the gravity of such a sin. By the way, it takes "two to tango", so you men involved in situations like this are just as liable.

John 13
¹⁵ "I have set you an example that you should do as I have done for you. ¹⁶I tell you the truth, no servant is greater than his master, nor is a messenger greater than the one who sent him. ¹⁷Now that you know these things, you will be blessed if you do them."

Hasn't the modern Christian church reversed the order in how we relate to Jesus? Hasn't the church made the servant <u>greater</u> than the master? The servants have somehow decided that living according to God's Holy Word is a matter of choice. The "messengers" (a.k.a. preachers) seem to have decided they are greater than the one who sent them. That's a bad idea.

John 10
³⁷ "Do not believe me unless I do what my Father does."

What if Christians out witnessing said, "Don't believe me unless I do what Jesus commands"? Wouldn't be much belief going around, would it? Let me ask you an important question: How many people have you known in your life that absolutely, positively lived a life Jesus would be proud of? Okay, tough question. How about this one: How many people have you known in your life who <u>almost always</u> exhibited the ways of Jesus? This is one of those questions we never think to ask ourselves, yet it may well be the most important question ever facing us. Many people will quickly respond, "Well, Jesus was a perfect person—he doesn't expect <u>us</u> to be perfect." I agree with both of these assertions—to a degree. Jesus was as close to perfect as any human will ever be, and I agree he doesn't expect us to be perfect, but....there's a big difference between perfection and premeditated failure. The average Christian is a walking, talking failure of what Christianity should be, so I must believe Jesus isn't a happy camper.

John 9
[40]Some Pharisees who were with him heard him say this and asked, "What? Are we blind too?"
[41]Jesus said, "If you were blind, you would not be guilty of sin; but now that you claim you can see, your guilt remains."

The Christian church of today claims they can see. They claim to know the teachings of Jesus Christ. If they were ignorant, God might cut them some slack, but by <u>claiming</u> they can see, they're making the statement they know what God wants from them. If they don't follow through on those commands, where does that leave them?

John 5
[39] "You diligently study the Scriptures because you think that by them you possess eternal life. These are the Scriptures that testify about me, [40]yet you refuse to come to me to have life."

I listen to Christian radio as I travel in my job, and I hear many hours of various preachers and speakers in a single week. One thing that always amuses me is the number of prophecy programs featuring callers who have some sort of new angle on the meaning of a passage in Revelation. Some of the hare-brained schemes I hear are laughable, but what's really sad is many of these well-meaning people spend little or no time studying the fundamentals of what Jesus taught, simply because they love the "advanced". It's akin to someone not graduating from the sixth grade, yet they spend hundreds of hours studying physics. Can they ultimately master physics? I suppose it's possible, but wouldn't it be much easier and more logical to acquire a foundational education first? I think it's important to remember Satan could quote Scripture quite well, but that certainly didn't mean he lived it. The Scriptures are given to us to lead us to Christ, not as some sort of adventure separate from Jesus. How many people brag, "I've read the Bible cover to cover at least 10 times"? Who cares? The only thing that matters is that you understand <u>and apply</u> what you've learned. I'd rather read and apply the book of Matthew than read the entire Bible simply as an educational exercise.

John 14
[12] "I tell you the truth, anyone who has faith in me will do what I have been doing. He will do even greater things than these, because I am going to the Father."

Is Jesus expecting us to perform miracles and drive out demons? According to Scripture, a true believer <u>could</u> indeed do these things, but I doubt most of us will ever have the faith and understanding to do them. What's clear is if we profess faith in Christ, there are many things we can and should do. Compassion and mercy are two action items each of us are capable of <u>if</u> we want to. Sadly, many of us are such selfish people and so hard-hearted we're unable to see the forest for the trees.

John 3
[19] "This is the verdict: Light has come into the world, but men loved darkness instead of light because their deeds were evil. [20]Everyone who does evil hates the light, and will not come into the light for fear that his deeds will be exposed. [21]But whoever lives by the truth comes into the light, so that it may be seen plainly that what he has done has been done through God."

Some will read this and say, "We can't work our way to Heaven", and they're right. We can, however, work towards living the life Jesus wants us to live. Living a "holy" life can't save any of us, but by living a holy life we can indeed become more observant of what Jesus taught us. **"But whoever lives by the truth comes into the light"**, in my opinion, could mean that a person living by "the rules" Jesus provided might put themselves in a better position to hear what Jesus is really telling them. In essence, it becomes a self-fulfilling prophecy. If you're a fisherman who wants to catch a marlin, do you cast your bait in a local pond?

John 7
[17] "If anyone chooses to do God's will, he will find out whether my teaching comes from God or whether I speak on my own."

Jesus is issuing a challenge to the reader in this passage. He's saying, "Check me out and see if the Father and I aren't one".

7

Instructions

◆

There's no need to guess

Galatians 2
[17] "If, while we seek to be justified in Christ, it becomes evident that we ourselves are sinners, does that mean that Christ promotes sin? Absolutely not! [18]If I rebuild what I destroyed, I prove that I am a lawbreaker."

I find this passage interesting since most preachers will explain to their congregation that as soon as a person accepts Jesus as their personal Savior, that person is justified. They even have a little saying that goes something like this: "When I believe in Jesus it's just-as-if-I'd never sinned." Paul seems to be saying justification is a process. A small point, perhaps, yet a point nonetheless. It sounds to me like justification is a journey in which we will sin at times, but the path should show progress. Some may point out that the journey is sanctification, but Paul used the term "justified".

Philippians 3
[10]I want to know Christ and the power of his resurrection and the fellowship of sharing in his sufferings, becoming like him in his death, [11]and so, somehow, to attain to the resurrection from the dead. [12]Not that I have already obtained all this, or have already been made perfect, but I press on to take hold of that for which Christ Jesus took hold of me.

Paul has been misconstrued as the "all grace" Apostle as long as I can remember. Paul was a man who certainly proclaimed the grace of Jesus Christ, but he was also a man who didn't take his Christianity lightly or for granted. The passage above vividly illustrates he continued to "work out his salvation". Do we?

1 Corinthians 9
²⁶Therefore I do not run like a man running aimlessly; I do not fight like a man beating the air. ²⁷No, I beat my body and make it my slave so that after I have preached to others, I myself will not be disqualified for the prize.

Here's yet another example of Paul's dedication to the job at hand. Most of the modern church is running aimlessly and sees nothing wrong with it. Read the "mission statements" of some churches and you'll see some outstanding examples of puffery and doubletalk.

1 Corinthians 11
¹Follow my example, as I follow the example of Christ.

There have been times I thought Paul's statement was arrogant, but if I really think about what he's saying, I must conclude he's trying to point out that despite his efforts to follow the example of Christ; he's still a long way from perfect. Paul doesn't fall back on "just believe", rather he clearly points out that fol-lowing the example of Christ is critical.

Ephesians 4
¹⁷So I tell you this, and insist on it in the Lord, that you must no longer live as the Gentiles do, in the futility of their thinking. ¹⁸They are darkened in their understanding and separated from the life of God because of the ignorance that is in them due to the hardening of their hearts. ¹⁹Having lost all sensitivity, they have given themselves over to sensuality so as to indulge in every kind of impurity, with a continual lust for more.
²⁰You, however, did not come to know Christ that way. ²¹Surely you heard of him and were taught in him in accordance with the truth that is in Jesus. ²²You were taught, with regard to your former way of life, to put off your old self, which is being corrupted by its deceitful desires; ²³to be made new in the attitude of your minds; ²⁴and to put on the new self, created to be like God in true righteousness and holiness.

Paul's teachings from Ephesians 4 reveal much more than "saved by Grace". Paul is writing to the Christian church in Ephesus, so he's dealing with "believers" just like most of us claim to be. Would you agree when Paul says, "(I) insist on it in the Lord", he's talking very seriously? I would tend to believe if Paul "insists on it in the Lord"; he's made a statement that this instruction is absolutely critical. I feel the modern Christian church has lost almost all sensitivity, and the results speak for themselves. For some unknown reason, many Christians honestly believe there is nothing they need to contribute to their Salvation process—all they do is sit back and let Jesus carry the full load. Make no mistake, Jesus <u>can</u> carry any load known to mankind, but that isn't the point. The point is that Jesus expects participation from the Salvation candidate in the process. We all know if a person has no "ownership" in something, his appreciation will be less than if he had to work for it. Salvation is no different—if we take an "easy come, easy go" attitude towards our priceless Salvation, we're heading for trouble. **"put off"** and **"put on"** are action phrases aimed squarely at us.

Philippians 3

[12]Not that I have already obtained all this, or have already been made perfect, but I press on to take hold of that for which Christ Jesus took hold of me. [13]Brothers, I do not consider myself yet to have taken hold of it. But one thing I do: Forgetting what is behind and straining toward what is ahead, [14]I press on toward the goal to win the prize for which God has called me heavenward in Christ Jesus.

[15]All of us who are mature should take such a view of things. And if on some point you think differently, that too God will make clear to you. [16]Only let us live up to what we have already attained.

[17]Join with others in following my example, brothers, and take note of those who live according to the pattern we gave you. [18]For, as I have often told you before and now say again even with tears, many live as enemies of the cross of Christ.

What could Paul be talking about in verse 12? It certainly sounds like Paul thinks he is still <u>in pursuit</u> of Salvation. Rather than mislead anyone, let's take a look at the pertinent verses <u>preceding</u> verse 12:

Philippians 3

[7]But whatever was to my profit I now consider loss for the sake of Christ. [8]What is more, I consider everything a loss compared to the surpassing greatness of knowing Christ Jesus my Lord, for whose sake I have lost all things. I consider them rubbish, that I may gain Christ [9]and be found in him, not having a righteousness of my own that comes from the law, but that which is through faith in Christ—the righteousness that comes from

God and is by faith. [10]**I want to know Christ and the power of his resurrection and the fellowship of sharing in his sufferings, becoming like him in his death,** [11]**and so, somehow, to attain to the resurrection from the dead.**

And so, Paul says in verse 12, **"Not that I have already obtained all this, or have already been made perfect, but I press on to take hold of that for which Christ Jesus took hold of me."** No matter how one slices and dices what Paul has clearly stated, how in the world can anyone even <u>suggest</u> Paul is in a complete state of sanctification <u>or</u> justification? He presses on, which tells us he has work to do. Not "saved by works", but rather <u>work to do</u> that Jesus Christ is compelling him to carry out. Jesus has given each of us jobs to do as well, but the modern church has all but written us a permission slip to continue to live a life of reckless abandon.

Acts 14
[22]**strengthening the disciples and encouraging them to remain true to the faith. "We must go through many hardships to enter the kingdom of God," they said.**

"We must go through many hardships to enter the kingdom of God". Contrast that with, "All you must do is believe." Were hardships only for the <u>early followers</u> of Christ? There's an old saying that goes, "Whatever doesn't kill you makes you stronger", and the pursuit of Jesus will always cause a true believer to suffer to some degree.

Ephesians 2
[1]**As for you, you were dead in your transgressions and sins,** [2]**in which you used to live when you followed the ways of this world and of the ruler of the kingdom of the air, the spirit who is now at work in those who are disobedient.** [3]**All of us also lived among them at one time, gratifying the cravings of our sinful nature and following its desires and thoughts. Like the rest, we were by nature objects of wrath.**

This passage talks much about "what was", rather than "what is". **"In which you <u>used</u> to live"**, **"…lived among them <u>at one time</u>"**, both signify the lives of the people changed. The modern church has perverted the Gospel to promise that people can live sinful lives, have an emotional moment and "walk the aisle", yet continue to live the same lifestyle with the promise of Salvation. Where is the repentance? Where is the change—profound <u>or</u> minor?

Hebrews 6
[11]We want each of you to show this same diligence to the very end, in order to make your hope sure. [12]We do not want you to become lazy, but to imitate those who through faith and patience inherit what has been promised.

Eternal security, also known as "once saved, always saved", has been a subject that makes me concerned, frightened and angry—all at the same time. I find nothing of substance in the Bible suggesting someone can't accept Jesus as Savior, and then reject Jesus a month or a year later. Eternal security believers will flippantly say, "Oh, a person like that was never really saved." When I read a passage like the one above, it becomes very clear we see conditions being established, and in this specific condition, we're told we need to do this (show diligence) **"in order to make your hope sure"**. The vast majority of church attendees (notice I refuse to call them Christians) have **"become lazy"** in their faith, and their spiritual leaders allow them to sit back and not have the least bit of concern about how they should be living.

1 John 2
[24]See that what you have heard from the beginning remains in you. If it does, you also will remain in the Son and in the Father. [25]And this is what he promised us—even eternal life.

"See that you're here at 8 AM tomorrow", says your boss. "Make sure you lock all of the doors since there have been burglaries in the neighborhood", says your wife. Are these suggestions? When someone tells me to "see that" or "make sure" something is done, I know they mean business. John says very clearly we need to **"see that what you have heard from the beginning remains in you."** What does that mean? Certainly the early church heard much in the way of teaching and instruction, so that covers quite a bit of ground. I believe this includes faith in Jesus Christ as our Savior, repentance, and a burning desire to live the type of life Jesus instructed us to live. **"If it does"** indicates anyone who has willfully rejected "what was heard" has set their own course of destruction. John's logic: If what we've heard doesn't remain in us, we won't remain in the Son and in the Father. If we aren't in the Son and in the Father, we're not bound for Heaven. Right?

James 1
¹²Blessed is the man who perseveres under trial, because when he has stood the test, he will receive the crown of life that God has promised to those who love him.

We often hear about the crown that will be bestowed upon the faithful who enter Heaven. I'm told that those who receive crowns will have a number of jewels in their crown corresponding to the life they've lead. I have some serious doubts about the validity of this premise, since we're all told there will be no envy in Heaven. If there really is no pride or no envy in Heaven, it wouldn't matter if we have a crown loaded with jewels or no crown at all. Be that as it may, the crown discussed above is the **"crown of life"**. In my opinion, this crown is needed for admittance into Heaven. How do we get one? The passage above tells us he **"who perseveres under trial"** will receive **"the crown of life that God has promised to those who love him."** Can you or I stand the test? What is the test? I personally think the test is daily life. What are our choices? Are they for God, or are they for man? If we simply make decisions without considering what God wants, we're failing the test, pure and simple.

Colossians 1
²¹Once you were alienated from God and were enemies in your minds because of your evil behavior. ²²But now he has reconciled you by Christ's physical body through death to present you holy in his sight, without blemish and free from accusation— ²³if you continue in your faith, established and firm, not moved from the hope held out in the gospel. This is the gospel that you heard and that has been proclaimed to every creature under heaven, and of which I, Paul, have become a servant.

If you only read verse 21 and 22, you could honestly walk away saying, "It looks to me like all I have to do is believe in Jesus as Savior". Then continue reading verse 23 and decide if the conditions change. **"If you continue in your faith"** is much more than simple belief. It's an active lifestyle the believer continues to adjust and refine, bringing that life into line with what Jesus wants. Does that sound like "working your way to Heaven"?

1 Corinthians 10
²¹**You cannot drink the cup of the Lord and the cup of demons too; you cannot have a part in both the Lord's table and the table of demons.** ²²**Are we trying to arouse the Lord's jealousy? Are we stronger than he?**

Paul is speaking to the Church at Corinth, and judging from his words, there are people in that church straying from the truth. Paul is very clear in his warning that **"you cannot have a part in both the Lord's table and the table of demons."** Read his words carefully—**"you cannot"** is the phrase he uses, not "it would be difficult". As Christians, we face daily choices in how we will or won't follow the instructions of Jesus.

Romans 6
¹**What shall we say, then? Shall we go on sinning so that grace may increase?** ²**By no means! We died to sin; how can we live in it any longer?**

Paul blows away any notion that "since sins are covered, there's no need to worry about them". The exclamation point behind **"By no means"** isn't there for the fun of it. Paul is serious about the situation and wants to let the people know exactly where he stands.

Romans 6
¹⁵**What then? Shall we sin because we are not under law but under grace? By no means!** ¹⁶**Don't you know that when you offer yourselves to someone to obey him as slaves, you are slaves to the one whom you obey—whether you are slaves to sin, which leads to death, or to obedience, which leads to righteousness?**

Just in case someone missed Paul's **"By no means"** the first time, he gives us a second coat in verse 15. Although I've heard this passage dozens of times in my life, it seems to always be presented from the pulpit as Paul saying, "You are saved by Grace, but you shouldn't sin". I think Paul's words are much stronger than that, as evidenced by the exclamation mark behind **"By no means"**. Read verse 16 again—are you a slave to sin or a slave to obedience? Look where each leads and reconsider if the answer isn't the right one.

Galatians 4
⁹But now that you know God—or rather are known by God—how is it that you are turning back to those weak and miserable principles? Do you wish to be enslaved by them all over again?

Perhaps Paul is using a play on words here to get the attention of the people in Galatia. There is a big difference between "knowing God" and being "known by God". God knows each and every person he ever created. That doesn't automatically guarantee he will save those people. When we really "know God", we're indicating we've studied what God requires of us, and we're making our intentions known that we intend to follow-through on what he's told us.

1 John 1
⁶If we claim to have fellowship with him yet walk in the darkness, we lie and do not live by the truth. ⁷But if we walk in the light, as he is in the light, we have fellowship with one another, and the blood of Jesus, his Son, purifies us from all sin.

I think this is one of the most powerful Scriptures in the New Testament. The Apostle John should qualify as one of the people closest to Jesus. It's unfortunate the Protestant religion wants to crown the Apostle Paul as their official spokesman even though the Apostle John probably spent more hours with Jesus than anyone else. John walked and talked with Jesus on a regular basis, hearing the teachings of Jesus first hand. John seldom minced words, and the passage above is certainly no exception. Verse 6 is a simple, yet strong warning to the "nominal" Christian. Let's read it again: **"If we claim to have fellowship with him yet walk in the darkness, we lie and do not live by the truth."** I meet people on a regular basis who "claim to have fellowship" with Jesus, yet their lives are devoid of any notable repentance and not only do they <u>not</u> love their fellow man, they have <u>no desire</u> to be able to love him. I find it tragically sad the average Christian church in America spends most of its time trying to let everyone know "Jesus accepts you just as you are", but seldom explains that Jesus also expects us to <u>change</u> after conversion. **"Walking in the darkness"** covers much ground, but what are some of the ways the average "carnal" Christian walks in darkness? **Alcohol and drug abusers**-While there are some people who are truly addicted and can't seem to break away from the deadly habit, many are simply "recreational users" that make an active choice to abuse the substances. **Liars**—Yes, I know "everyone" lies, but there are differences between the "little white-lie" and the habitual, calculated lie. I've recently been able to see a couple of people who are professional liars. They lie so much and so often that even when they have the opportunity to tell the truth they still choose to lie. Liars are never able to rest, since they must keep their mind going full-steam to be sure they can remember what they've already lied about to keep their next lie consistent. Once again, making an active daily choice to engage in untruthful behavior is premeditated sin and is "walking in the darkness". The group I'm most concerned about is racists. I believe there will be many "good Christians" who will ultimately find themselves in Hell for one simple reason: they chose to hate people of races different than their own. It doesn't matter how many dollars they've given to the church, doesn't matter how many Sunday School classes they've taught, doesn't matter how many good deeds they've done—hatred of others without any reason other than skin color is, in my opinion, a one-way ticket to Hell. One of my most vivid memories in the church happened around 1999 when I was asked to fill-in for our pastor one Sunday. The topic of my sermon was, of all things, racism. My "rubber meets the road" line was simple and it went something like this: "I would really hate to think some good, hard-working people in this church would one day wind up in Hell because they didn't love their brothers and sisters of other colors." After the sermon, one elderly gentleman came up to me, wiping the tears from his eyes, and said, "John, I needed to hear that." That man, in my opinion, was one of the most kind and loving men in our church, but apparently he had a problem loving those different than himself. It would have been very easy to preach a sermon that would have been yet another "don't worry, be happy" message that doesn't step on any toes and doesn't make anyone squirm in their seats. Sermons like that have their place, but sometimes the pastor needs to lay it on the line and not worry about who gets uneasy.

Galatians 5
16So I say, live by the Spirit, and you will not gratify the desires of the sinful nature. 17For the sinful nature desires what is contrary to the Spirit, and the Spirit what is contrary to the sinful nature. They are in conflict with each other, so that you do not do what you want. 18But if you are led by the Spirit, you are not under law.

"If" is a tiny word in terms of length, yet the ramifications of the word are enormous. "If" you are led by the Spirit, you are not under law. I might also point out Paul is once again issuing instructions to the church in how they should live. How Paul has been heralded as the "all grace" apostle is beyond me. Paul frequently spoke of how Christians should live, and how people who don't live by those standards should question whether they're really saved. Since he's specifically talking to the church at Galatia, one might assume it's safe to say everyone in the church is truly saved, but when Paul says, "if you are led by the Spirit", he's telling everyone to check their Salvation. We need more of that today, but many consider it to be "negative" in our present world. As I've said before, there's good news and bad news. The bad news is that millions of people who think they're Christians will end up in Hell. The good news is that until they get there, their self-esteem will be in fine condition.

1 Thessalonians 4
³It is God's will that you should be sanctified: that you should avoid sexual immorality; ⁴that each of you should learn to control his own body in a way that is holy and honorable, ⁵not in passionate lust like the heathen, who do not know God; ⁶and that in this matter no one should wrong his brother or take advantage of him. The Lord will punish men for all such sins, as we have already told you and warned you. ⁷For God did not call us to be impure, but to live a holy life. ⁸Therefore, he who rejects this instruction does not reject man but God, who gives you his Holy Spirit.

Paul's issued some stern advice and warnings to the church at Thessalonica. Look at his choice of words carefully: **"each of you should learn to control his own body"** since those who don't **"do not know God"**. It's clear to me Paul isn't saying that accepting Jesus will rid the believer's life of such things—the believer has a role in cleaning up their own lives. Verse 8 is the real kicker, though: **"Therefore, he who rejects this instruction does not reject man but God, who gives you his Holy Spirit."** In my mind, this statement is an open and shut case against those who willingly reject the teachings and commandments of God. If we reject God, what does that do to our eternity? I firmly believe rejection of God is an automatic ticket to Hell. Can anyone argue this point? For those of you who would like to believe a Christian doesn't have to "do" anything, read the passage again and notice when Paul says, "you should", "you should", "no one should", which certainly indicates these are action-items for a professing Christian.

Philippians 2
¹²Therefore, my dear friends, as you have always obeyed—not only in my presence, but now much more in my absence—continue to work out your

salvation with fear and trembling, ¹³for it is God who works in you to will and to act according to his good purpose.

If Salvation is a one-time, "got-it/don't-got-it" condition, why would Paul tell the Philippians to **"continue to work out your salvation with fear and trembling"**? How many people today ever have a "fear and trembling" session with God? Not many, I'm afraid, since the good old pastor tells them every week that everything is fine. Pastor is Hell-bound, and he's got a big part of his congregation handcuffed to him. It's a sad thing.

Romans 8
¹²Therefore, brothers, we have an obligation—but it is not to the sinful nature, to live according to it. ¹³For if you live according to the sinful nature, you will die; but if by the Spirit you put to death the misdeeds of the body, you will live, ¹⁴because those who are led by the Spirit of God are sons of God.

If we use "John's logic" we can see that Scripture says, **"those who are led by the Spirit of God are sons of God"**, therefore "those who are not led by the Spirit of God are not sons of God", right? Pushing the logic envelope a bit further, can we say "those who aren't sons of God <u>are</u> sons of Satan?" God gave us the Holy Spirit as an agent of change that can clean up every square inch of our lives. Try this little exercise: If you can be honest and acknowledge a problem in your Christian walk, such as worship of material things, go to God and ask him to send the Holy Spirit to rid you of that affliction. If you don't want to call the Holy Spirit in, you're now taking full responsibility for your rebellion. God has promised the Holy Spirit can make the change, but you must be willing to accept his help. Let's use this example: A young married man with children loves the "finer things in life". So much so that he's up to his neck in debt. The financial stress is taking a toll on his marriage, but the lure of buying a seventy-thousand-dollar speedboat is too strong to walk away from. This is a classic case crying out for the help of the Holy Spirit. This man can simply send up a prayer to God asking for help in beating the "gotta have it" syndrome. If this man honestly values his wife and family more than material things, he will gladly accept God's offer to send the Holy Spirit. I know this works, and I also know if you really <u>don't want</u> the help, God won't force it on you. All I can say is this: if someone knows they're living in a way unpleasing to God, and if that person is given a way around their sinful life and chooses to reject the offer, they're playing with fire.

James 1
²⁶If anyone considers himself religious and yet does not keep a tight rein on his tongue, he deceives himself and his religion is worthless.

Now things start to get personal. How many "Good Christians" do you know who gossip until the cows come home? Of all the sinful habits the Holy Spirit has helped me overcome, control of my tongue is the one that seems to resist any discipline. Could it be that the toughest sins to overcome are the ones we're most proficient in? I'm good at debating, and I'm good at pushing my point of view when I need to. While there's nothing wrong with either skill, using those skills on people who clearly don't have a chance is wrong. The sins of the tongue can manifest themselves in other ways as well, such as lying and being profane. I'm happy that my use of profanity is a tiny fraction of what it used to be, but that's not good enough. The Holy Spirit is working on that every day. I may still slip up and use one of the more minor profanities, but each time I do, I feel that little twinge. Lying has never been much of a problem for me—in fact, my love for the truth is what really gets me in the most trouble. Being truthful in a world that has a hard time separating truth from fiction is difficult. Surveys have shown most Americans lie. Consider, for a moment, America is a "Christian Nation". That said, we apparently have plenty of Christians who lie and think nothing of it, and that's a sad commentary, folks.

1 Thessalonians 3
⁵For this reason, when I could stand it no longer, I sent Timothy to find out about your faith. I was afraid that in some way the tempter might have tempted you and our efforts might have been useless.

In our modern times, people get mad if you question their faith. Consider that during the Apostle Paul's time, the church was about as strong as it ever was. If faith was a problem then, you can only imagine what we face 2000 years later. Paul wanted to "find out" about their faith, and sent Timothy to gather the data. How does this action align with the "once saved, always saved" doctrine? I think we need some modern day Timothy's to check out just what the level of faith is in our churches. Some "scholars" will try to twist this passage into saying "the church members in Thessalonica were really saved, but their rewards in Heaven might be limited". Hogwash—read the whole passage: **"and our efforts might have been useless"**. Was Paul talking about his efforts to help the church have plenty of rewards in Heaven? I don't think so—he's talking about <u>getting</u> the church to Heaven.

Acts 10

³⁴Then Peter began to speak: "I now realize how true it is that God does not show favoritism ³⁵but accepts men from every nation who fear him and do what is right."

"Favoritism" can be defined here in a number of ways, but I tend to believe Peter is talking about the various flavors of Christian churches. As the apostles fanned out across the region, they probably had some minor differences in how they proclaimed the Gospel of Jesus Christ. What I think Peter is pointing out is that we should "fear" or more accurately, have a healthy respect for God—<u>including</u> fear if necessary, and do what's right. The average Christian seems to be brain-dead when it comes to doing what's right. Cheating on taxes, speeding, withholding benefits to employees while living a life of luxury, among other things, is certainly not "doing what is right". Go make your own list. If you can't, then you'll need to recruit the Holy Spirit to give you a conscience, because none of us lead blameless lives.

Titus 2

¹¹For the grace of God that brings salvation has appeared to all men. ¹²It teaches us to say "No" to ungodliness and worldly passions, and to live self-controlled, upright and godly lives in this present age,

Do our modern Christian denominations teach us to say "No" to ungodliness and worldly passions? Do they teach us to live self-controlled, upright and godly lives? I'd have to say overall, the modern church doesn't teach us what Titus 2:11-12 addressed. If anyone gets in the pulpit today and starts talking about self-control or discipline, the congregation might rebel and shout "legalist!" whenever any change for the better is suggested by the speaker. What does the average "Christian" want to hear in a sermon? Jesus died for past, present and future sins. As long as you "believe" in Jesus, you'll go to Heaven.

Hebrews 10
> ¹⁶ "This is the covenant I will make with them
>   after that time, says the Lord.
> I will put my laws in their hearts,
>   and I will write them on their minds."

Here's another "John's logic" question: If the Lord says he will make a covenant with us, and if he says he will put his laws in our hearts, and write them on our minds, do the people who <u>don't have</u> God's law in their hearts and <u>don't have</u> them written on their minds have possession of God's covenant?

2 Corinthians 5
¹⁵**And he died for all, that those who live should no longer live for themselves but for him who died for them and was raised again.**

Here's a nice passage that gives us reassurance Jesus died for everyone, but closely following that promise is a qualifier: **"that those who live should no longer live for themselves but for him who died for them and was raised again."** Let's look at this from an earthly perspective. Let's say you needed a kidney transplant and only one person in the world could provide that kidney. Without the transplant, you will die. Although your lifestyle has been somewhat unsavory, the donor's life is one of sacrifice and love for fellow man. The donor isn't demanding you be just like him, he's just asking you to do your best to love others and share what you have. It's real simple—the donor is saying, "Look, just clean up your act and I'll give you a kidney so you can go on to live a full life." What would most people say to that request? "I'll do it!" How then, can we expect to receive <u>eternal</u> life while not living the life Jesus calls us to live? I don't think the average Christian takes time to consider what eternity is. We're so preoccupied with our short existence on this earth that we don't even consider the length and breadth of eternity.

Ephesians 2
⁸**For it is by grace you have been saved, through faith—and this not from yourselves, it is the gift of God— ⁹not by works, so that no one can boast. ¹⁰For we are God's workmanship, created in Christ Jesus to do good works, which God prepared in advance for us to do.**

I always find it amusing that "saved by Grace" people will very quickly quote Ephesians 2:8-9 as a way of saying, "We don't have to do anything but believe". They will also remind me God wisely provided Grace free of charge so anyone could have it, regardless of their station in life. That's all fine and good, but read on: **"For we are God's workmanship, created in Christ Jesus to do good works, which God prepared in advance for us to do."** John's logic: If someone doesn't do good works, are they really God's workmanship?

Romans 15
[15]I have written you quite boldly on some points, as if to remind you of them again, because of the grace God gave me [16]to be a minister of Christ Jesus to the Gentiles with the priestly duty of proclaiming the gospel of God, so that the Gentiles might become an offering acceptable to God, sanctified by the Holy Spirit.

Most of the persons reading this are "Gentiles". What is Paul saying in the passage above? Paul proclaims the gospel of God so the Gentiles might become an offering acceptable to God, sanctified by the Holy Spirit. If the "gospel of God" is the same as "the Gospel of Jesus Christ", then we're presented with that gospel to illustrate how we need to change our lives to follow Jesus. If God sees no intention on our part to change, and if he isn't getting any request from us to send us the Holy Spirit, are we an offering acceptable to God? I think not.

John 14
[26] "But the Counselor, the Holy Spirit, whom the Father will send in my name, will teach you all things and will remind you of everything I have said to you."

The Holy Spirit makes yet another appearance in the Gospels, reminding us once more that he is available for every Christian who needs help with their lives. I seldom hear anything these days about the Holy Spirit, and if I do, it's mostly in passing. At the risk of beating the same drum over and over again, let's read what the role of the Holy Spirit is: to **"teach you all things and will remind you of everything I** (Jesus) **have said to you."** Isn't that incredibly powerful? What a wonderful earthly resource Jesus provides for us in his absence. I find it tragically sad the average Christian simply believes Jesus died and was resurrected and that until we meet him again, we have nothing but the written word to connect to him. The Holy Spirit is very much alive and with us every minute of the day…that is, if we <u>want</u> him to be.

Romans 8

[5]Those who live according to the sinful nature have their minds set on what that nature desires; but those who live in accordance with the Spirit have their minds set on what the Spirit desires.

If you have your mind "set" on something, what does that mean? For most of us, it means we've considered all the costs and have decided whatever we have our mind set on is more important than the conditions that accompany the pursuit of that particular thing. In other words, we have a premeditated action toward possessing it. The sinful nature, then, is something that many "set their minds on" to accommodate. That's a dangerous thing, folks. Compare those people to the ones who have their mind "set" on what the <u>Spirit</u> desires. Which person do you think God smiles upon? Let me rephrase that: Is God smiling on the people in Hell?

Romans 14

[10]You, then, why do you judge your brother? Or why do you look down on your brother? For we will all stand before God's judgment seat. [11]It is written:

"'As surely as I live,' says the Lord,
'every knee will bow before me;
every tongue will confess to God.'" [12]So then, each of us will give an account of himself to God.

Many Christians are taught when they become saved, "God remembers their sins no more". Perhaps <u>past</u> sins are forgotten in the Salvation process, but it certainly sounds like God is indeed keeping tabs on what we do <u>after</u> conversion. Isn't it completely fair that God <u>does</u> keep up with what we've done? People are motivated by all sorts of things, but avoiding punishment is a motivator most human beings share. Giving an account to God is something a vital, practicing Christian should look forward to, not dread.

2 Thessalonians 3

[6]In the name of the Lord Jesus Christ, we command you, brothers, to keep away from every brother who is idle and does not live according to the teaching you received from us.

Whenever I read this, I think about a Christian friend of mine. He loves the Lord and is a truly good person, but on the job he's about as lazy as they come. He's been fired from a number of companies, yet his work ethic apparently hasn't improved. While I do believe he's a Christian, his witness is compromised by the way he conducts himself at work. Most people will disagree with me on my view of this topic, and that's okay. I think anyone who <u>says</u> they're a Christian yet doesn't provide their employer with an honest day's work for a day's pay doesn't hold up their end of the bargain. A person active in theft is not only compromising their witness, they may be compromising their eternity.

1 Timothy 5
[20]Those who sin are to be rebuked publicly, so that the others may take warning.
[21]I charge you, in the sight of God and Christ Jesus and the elect angels, to keep these instructions without partiality, and to do nothing out of favoritism.
[22]Do not be hasty in the laying on of hands, and do not share in the sins of others. Keep yourself pure.

At the risk of sounding like a broken record, I'll point out that the Apostle Paul, the "Apostle of Grace" as some see him, is offering specific instructions to the church. What would happen today if a church publicly rebuked members who have sinned? Plenty of people would leave the church, citing the "lack of love and compassion". Perhaps the greatest love and compassion we can show for others <u>is</u> to point out their sins and have them point out <u>ours</u>. The modern church wants to pussyfoot around this situation and not deal with it for obvious reasons. Is Paul just kidding around? When he says, **"I charge you, in the sight of God and Christ Jesus and the elect angels"**, does it sound like he's joking? I'm not familiar with what Paul is talking about in regards to the laying on of hands, but my study Bible says he's referring to the ordination of church elders. Whether it's elders or deacons, the church needs to tighten up their policy on who they choose to represent them. I've known some deacons who had all sorts of skeletons in their closets that wouldn't have been hard to find if someone would have done their homework. Should a deacon be perfect? There are no perfect people, but there are often better choices for deacon if the church will look around just a little.

2 Corinthians 7

¹Since we have these promises, dear friends, let us purify ourselves from everything that contaminates body and spirit, perfecting holiness out of reverence for God.

When you read the words, **"let us purify ourselves…"**, do you walk away thinking you have <u>no</u> personal responsibility? These are action words, meant to tell us we have a role in the cleanup of our lives. Can we do a total cleanup? Of course not—if we could we wouldn't need Jesus. What the average Christian fails to realize is each of us has a very vital role in the sanctification process. We're such a spoiled and coddled people that we think we just need to sit back and wait for someone to do our dirty work for us. Take a look around at the car washes in your town—very few people ever wash their cars anymore. Quick oil changes, tanning booths, fingernail shops—they're all signs of the times we do less and less ourselves and expect more "services" to be provided for our comfort. If we don't avoid body and spiritual "contamination", we're asking for trouble.

1 John 3

³Everyone who has this hope in him purifies himself, just as he is pure.

Here's yet another passage that speaks some action words, **"purifies himself"**. Someone out there might rebut: "Oh, but what John means is when we have hope in Jesus, we automatically purify ourselves." It looks to me like the passage could go either way, so since it's your eternity, make it easy on yourself.

2 Corinthians 6

¹⁷ "Therefore come out from them and be separate, says the Lord. Touch no unclean thing, and I will receive you."

This passage should certainly need no explanation, but apparently folks just don't understand Christians are called to leave their life of filth and destruction. Perhaps the biggest problem today is many Christians converted at a young age, and never really considered most of the people around us we imitate might well be disciples of Satan. If there's one key problem in the Christian church today, it would have to be the fact most Christians don't live a life any different than the lost. That's a shame.

1 Timothy 4
[16]Watch your life and doctrine closely. Persevere in them, because if you do, you will save both yourself and your hearers.

Perseverance is a topic seldom taught these days. Once again, I think the main culprit may be the common practice of conversion at an early age. If a lost person gets saved at 30 years of age, they can look back on a sinful life and see the dividing line between what they <u>were</u> and what they are <u>now</u>. When kids "get saved" at 12 years old, they don't really understand what sin is about—they're just too young to comprehend what they consider to be bad as a kid will be inconsequential once they become adults. Perseverance is all about taking responsibility for our own actions <u>after</u> conversion. Taking responsibility is something not taught very much anymore. Just this past Sunday, my pastor was telling a story about being pulled over for speeding. By his own admission, he was driving "very fast". When the policeman recognized him, he apologized for stopping him and didn't issue a ticket. The congregation laughed and thought it was a funny story. I find it tragic a pastor wouldn't tell the officer, "thanks for recognizing me, but I <u>was</u> breaking the law, so please do your duty and write the ticket". The rules, it seems, are always for other people, never for ourselves.

1 Thessalonians 5
[4]But you, brothers, are not in darkness so that this day should surprise you like a thief. [5]You are all sons of the light and sons of the day. We do not belong to the night or to the darkness. [6]So then, let us not be like others, who are asleep, but let us be alert and self-controlled.

I think the key phrase here is **"let us be alert and self-controlled"**. Should it have read, "let us say that we believe"? There is an emphasis on the role of the believer, and that's appropriate.

1 Corinthians 5
[9]I have written you in my letter not to associate with sexually immoral people— [10]not at all meaning the people of this world who are immoral, or the greedy and swindlers, or idolaters. In that case you would have to leave this world. [11]But now I am writing you that you must not associate with anyone who calls himself a brother but is sexually immoral or greedy, an idolater or a slanderer, a drunkard or a swindler. With such a man do not even eat.

How many "good Christians" hang-out with people they shouldn't? How many church deacons can be found at "sports-bars" like Hooters? Call me a prude, but no Christian man has any business visiting Hooters. Hooter's method of operation is far too obvious for anyone to be fooled, and once again, Christians are called to a higher standard. If a person claims Christianity yet walks in the darkness, it might well be they need to check their relationship with Jesus Christ. Will every Christian stumble and do things that displease Christ? Certainly, but visiting bars and restaurants featuring scantily-clad women is a premeditated action that leaves no room for "it was an accident" excuses. I find it interesting Paul is telling us our association with the lost of the world isn't his main concern, rather he is more concerned with our association with people who <u>claim</u> to be Christians but really aren't. Paul says if a man calls himself a brother, yet his actions prove otherwise, stay away from him. I had to make a hard decision some time back to discontinue a long-time friendship with a person who claimed to be a brother, yet some issues in his life proved otherwise. I still miss him, although I know I did what needed to be done. Some well-meaning folks might say, "John, that guy might have needed your friendship to pull him away from the bad choices he was making." Perhaps, but sometimes when we're trying to pull someone <u>up</u>, what ultimately happens is <u>they pull us down</u>. A story ran on the news today that told of a construction worker who took a break to cool off in a small lake, swam out a little ways and went under. Another worker, who was a good swimmer, swam out to rescue him, and before it was over <u>both</u> men drowned. People who are drowning will sometimes pull their rescuer under, so we must be careful.

James 2

[14]**What good is it, my brothers, if a man claims to have faith but has no deeds? Can such faith save him? [15]Suppose a brother or sister is without clothes and daily food. [16]If one of you says to him, "Go, I wish you well; keep warm and well fed," but does nothing about his physical needs, what good is it?**

James might well have been the original creator of the popular saying, "If you're going to talk the talk, then walk the walk". It's unfortunate so many Christians want to talk about the love of God through Jesus Christ, then turn right around and laughingly talk about the death penalty (fry 'em!), or killing our enemies in war (nuke 'em!). Where is the love? Some Christians reading this will say, "Oh, we're only required to love our brothers and sisters in Christ". And people call <u>me</u>

a legalist. Even if that premise would hold water, a question still remains: Are you concerned about people on death row and people we're fighting in war.........if they're Christians?

James 4
[7]Submit yourselves, then, to God. Resist the devil, and he will flee from you. [8]Come near to God and he will come near to you. Wash your hands, you sinners, and purify your hearts, you double-minded. [9]Grieve, mourn and wail. Change your laughter to mourning and your joy to gloom. [10]Humble yourselves before the Lord, and he will lift you up.

I think James was wise to list **"Submit yourselves, then, to God"** prior to saying, **"Resist the devil, and he will flee from you."** Why? Satan, like any good businessman, will weigh out the cost of his efforts in relationship to their return. In theory, if someone resists Satan, we erroneously assume Satan will say, "Gee, he's tough, I think I'll move on to someone else that's easier." When we submit ourselves to God, we're going to God for our battle armor prior to receiving attacks from Satan. Without the full armor of God, we're not likely to be able to survive an attack from Satan. It's certainly not hard to understand the concept of: **"Come near to God and he come near to you"**. The "positive thinking" among us won't appreciate James instructions to "grieve, mourn and wail", and to change laughter to mourning and their joy to gloom. Why? Because it's hard for positive thinking people to humble themselves. It's usually "all about them", and humility is a characteristic often considered to be a weakness in our American society. I personally think humility must be a major characteristic of a Christian, otherwise we'd want to put ourselves on a level too close to where God resides, and that will never happen in God's kingdom. There are three action words in this passage that should be studied closely: 1. **Submit**, 2. **Purify**, 3. **Humble**. It's not rocket science, is it?

2 Timothy 2
[19]Nevertheless, God's solid foundation stands firm, sealed with this inscription: "The Lord knows those who are his," and, "Everyone who confesses the name of the Lord must turn away from wickedness."

Long after the resurrection, Paul wrote the words above. Do you find anything that says, "Just believe"? The action on the believer's part is clear-cut and simple: **"Everyone who confesses the name of the Lord must turn away from wicked-**

ness." Why have we strayed so far from the concept the Christian has a <u>job</u> to do while on this earth? Why have we simply dismissed personal sin as a "well, it's bound to happen" type thing? Why do we re-crucify Christ over and over again for the hundreds of sins we commit <u>knowingly</u> and <u>willfully</u>? I think the answer is quite simple: the average Christian is lazy and unmotivated to make any change in their life simply because their pastor is telling them their past, present and future sins are forgiven. "Don't worry, be happy!"

Romans 6

¹²Therefore do not let sin reign in your mortal body so that you obey its evil desires. ¹³Do not offer the parts of your body to sin, as instruments of wickedness, but rather offer yourselves to God, as those who have been brought from death to life; and offer the parts of your body to him as instruments of righteousness.

I love using the words of Paul, "the all-grace man" to remind people he had much more to say about personal responsibility than he did about living a carefree life. Some folks might get confused and think Paul was speaking to unbelievers, but Paul's letters to the various churches were indeed written to believers. The Gospel had already been explained many times to the recipients of these letters, so Paul's words above are words of instruction to <u>believers</u>. Did Paul think the church members could be sin-free? Of course not, but what he <u>is</u> saying is "clean-up your own act".

Ephesians 5

¹⁵Be very careful, then, how you live—not as unwise but as wise, ¹⁶making the most of every opportunity, because the days are evil. ¹⁷Therefore do not be foolish, but understand what the Lord's will is.

Very few of us make the most of every opportunity, and if we do, it's as the world defines "opportunity". How many Christians know what the Lord's will is? I suppose a typical answer might be, "the Lord wants everyone to be saved". Perhaps, but is that the <u>only</u> desire of the Lord? Think about this for a moment—if God's people would do precisely what God wants, what would that be? I tend to think God's wishes are much more pragmatic than what the average Christian believes. Many Christians think God is happiest when we're sitting around praising him and worshipping him. That, I think is mistaken thinking. Why? God, unlike humans, has no ego. God doesn't need to be stroked, rather it is simply good and appropriate for us to honor and worship him. So what would make God happy if adoration is "optional" for him? I feel a practical application of our Christian education is very important to God. Can God snap his mighty fingers and wipe out poverty and hunger in the world? Of course, but history shows God's major miracles in areas like this aren't happening today as in Biblical times. God empowers his people to be his eyes, his hands and his feet. Let's put this situation into something humans can relate to—suppose a man is very benevolent and is always working hard to help the poor and downtrodden. That man might one day reach a point in which he is no longer able to perform the services he loves to provide, but he has children. He's taught his children very well about the merits of helping others and they know exactly what to do. Now, ask yourself this question: "Would this man be happier hearing his children talk about what should be done to help others, or would he be happier if they do something to help others? Modern Christianity has largely become a religion of people who focus more on theory rather than the practice of their faith. Knowing every Scripture is of little value if a person's Christianity isn't dynamic.

2 Timothy 2
16Avoid godless chatter, because those who indulge in it will become more and more ungodly.

I often engage in "godless chatter", and I pray God will help me with this problem. Why do we do this? I tend to believe people feel like silence somehow suggests a lack of friendliness, so what do we do? Yak, yak, yak. When it gets right down to it, there isn't much to talk about other than what other people are doing, and that's where the problem begins. Human nature, being what it is, contributes to the problem. For instance: your conversation partner starts talking about another person in complementary terms. You're likely to relate what you think is good about that person as well, right? Sadly, few conversations talk about the merits of others, rather we tend to focus on weaknesses. Why is that? Perhaps we feel better about ourselves after we bash others, but does that really work? I think not. I almost always walk away from conversations like this feeling as though I need to take a shower. The passage above tells why—"those who indulge in it (godless chatter) will become more and more ungodly."

2 Corinthians 13
11Finally, brothers, good-by. Aim for perfection, listen to my appeal, be of one mind, live in peace. And the God of love and peace will be with you.

How many Christians aim for perfection? "But John, Christians aren't perfect, just forgiven". Yes, I've heard that a few thousand times in my life, but why do Christians feel they can sit back and do nothing to enrich their relationship with Jesus? Beats me. Paul tells us very clearly if we aim for perfection, "**the God of love and peace will be with you.**" Who wouldn't want that?

1 Timothy 6
[11]But you, man of God, flee from all this, and pursue righteousness, godliness, faith, love, endurance and gentleness.

What is Paul talking about when he says, "flee from all this"? Let's back up to verse 3 and read from there:

[3]If anyone teaches false doctrines and does not agree to the sound instruction of our Lord Jesus Christ and to godly teaching, [4]he is conceited and understands nothing. He has an unhealthy interest in controversies and quarrels about words that result in envy, strife, malicious talk, evil suspicions [5]and constant friction between men of corrupt mind, who have been robbed of the truth and who think that godliness is a means to financial gain.
[6]But godliness with contentment is great gain. [7]For we brought nothing into the world, and we can take nothing out of it. [8]But if we have food and clothing, we will be content with that. [9]People who want to get rich fall into temptation and a trap and into many foolish and harmful desires that plunge men into ruin and destruction. [10]For the love of money is a root of all kinds of evil. Some people, eager for money, have wandered from the faith and pierced themselves with many griefs.

While Paul specifically mentions money, he doesn't limit his concerns to financial issues. Let's take a close look at Paul's warning in verse 3: **"If anyone teaches false doctrines and does not agree to the sound instruction of our Lord Jesus Christ and to godly teaching, he is conceited and understands nothing."** "**Understands nothing**" is a pretty heavy assessment of the person in question. Does this mean the person doesn't understand Salvation? Not necessarily, but I wouldn't rule that out. What are some other traits of the person who "understands nothing"? They have an unhealthy interest in controversies and want to get rich. Although being rich isn't a sin in itself, please show me someone who is rich that didn't do some things along the way that compromised their Christian walk.

1 Peter 5
[8]Be self-controlled and alert. Your enemy the devil prowls around like a roaring lion looking for someone to devour.

Peter often writes about the practical side of Christianity. "Be self-controlled and alert" is yet another action phrase that reminds us our walk with the Lord is more than being on theological cruise-control.

Romans 13
[13]Let us behave decently, as in the daytime, not in orgies and drunkenness, not in sexual immorality and debauchery, not in dissension and jealousy. [14]Rather, clothe yourselves with the Lord Jesus Christ, and do not think about how to gratify the desires of the sinful nature.

"Let us behave decently" suggests we <u>are</u> capable. "As in the daytime" implies we shouldn't think we can behave publicly one way, and then differently under other circumstances. "Clothe yourselves" indicates we have a choice, and "do not think about how to gratify" reminds us to keep our noses clean. Paul once again shows us we have choices and should take an active role in our Christian walk, rather than the "all grace" persona he has unfairly been given.

1 John 3
[10]This is how we know who the children of God are and who the children of the devil are: Anyone who does not do what is right is not a child of God; nor is anyone who does not love his brother.

Can a Christian sometimes do something that isn't right or not always love his brother? Sure, it's possible, but these situations should be extremely rare <u>and</u> on the decrease. People who, on a regular basis, do wrong and refuse to love their brother need to question their Christianity.

Colossians 3
[1]Since, then, you have been raised with Christ, set your hearts on things above, where Christ is seated at the right hand of God. [2]Set your minds on things above, not on earthly things. [3]For you died, and your life is now hid-

den with Christ in God. ⁴When Christ, who is your life, appears, then you also will appear with him in glory.
⁵Put to death, therefore, whatever belongs to your earthly nature: sexual immorality, impurity, lust, evil desires and greed, which is idolatry. ⁶Because of these, the wrath of God is coming. ⁷You used to walk in these ways, in the life you once lived. ⁸But now you must rid yourselves of all such things as these: anger, rage, malice, slander, and filthy language from your lips.

We hear some promises in the passage above with the words, **"Since, then, you have been raised with Christ"**, and **"your life is now hidden with Christ in God"**. If we feel we deserve to be included with these followers of Christ, let's look at some of the challenges that lie in front of us. **"Put to death"** is an action phrase that expects fulfillment from the Christian. Put to death what? **"Whatever belongs to your earthly nature"**, but specifically: **"sexual immorality, impurity, lust, evil desires and greed"**. And what can we expect if these things aren't put to death? **"The wrath of God"**. It's extremely easy for the "just believe" crowd to simply dismiss these instructions by announcing, "Jesus died for my sins", and although you'll get no argument from me on that subject, what is our role? Can we murder someone and simply say, "Jesus covered that"? Of course not, but will Jesus forgive us for saying an unkind word in a heated moment? I think he will, but I also believe Jesus is expecting us to pay more attention when our tempers flare and he also expects us to avoid situations in which we get angry. The passage tells us that **"you used to walk in these ways, in the life you once lived"**. Can we agree **"you used to walk in these ways"** means that these sins were a common way of life? If these same sins are still common, what does that say about the health of the person's Christianity?

John 12
²⁶ **"Whoever serves me must follow me; and where I am, my servant also will be. My Father will honor the one who serves me."**

This is one of those passages that defies the hearer to define it in a way other than intended: **"Where I am, my servant will also be"**. How can a "Christian" read this and say, "Well, righteousness is fine for Jesus Christ, but heck, let's be practical here". We are a people who are so intelligent, so enlightened, that we believe we've somehow become smarter than God himself. That might amuse God if it weren't for the final, deadly situation we put ourselves in.

Romans 16
²⁵Now to him who is able to establish you by my gospel and the proclamation of Jesus Christ, according to the revelation of the mystery hidden for long ages past, ²⁶but now revealed and made known through the prophetic writings by the command of the eternal God, so that all nations might believe and obey him—

Here we see the important connection: "believe" <u>and</u> "obey". "The Apprentice" can <u>believe</u> Donald Trump will give him a job that will pay a million dollars a year, but unless he obeys Trump's orders, the chance of that happening is slim to none. Conversely, why would Jesus want to offer Salvation to those who refuse to do what he asks?

1 Corinthians 15
³³Do not be misled: "Bad company corrupts good character." ³⁴Come back to your senses as you ought, and stop sinning; for there are some who are ignorant of God—I say this to your shame.

Paul might well be telling many of us to check out who we associate with. It's very difficult to hang out with liars and crooks and not have some of that rub off on us. When we "come back to our senses" and "stop sinning", will we really cease sinning completely? I don't see anything Scripturally telling me we can ever be totally free from sin, but I certainly believe it should be the goal of every Christian to be working towards a sin-free life. How close can we get? Honestly, I don't know. Perhaps I should turn that question around and ask, "How much can you sin and still go to Heaven?" Can anyone answer that?

Colossians 1
¹⁰And we pray this in order that you may live a life worthy of the Lord and may please him in every way: bearing fruit in every good work, growing in the knowledge of God, ¹¹being strengthened with all power according to his glorious might so that you may have great endurance and patience, and joyfully ¹²giving thanks to the Father, who has qualified you to share in the inheritance of the saints in the kingdom of light.

We read in this passage that God qualifies us to **"share in the inheritance of the saints in the kingdom of light"**. <u>God</u> qualifies us, we don't qualify ourselves. What does God use in this qualification process? He looks to see if we're living a life worthy of the Lord. He wants to see if we're pleasing him in every way. He looks to see if we're bearing fruit in every good work and that we're growing in our knowledge of him. As he sees these things, we're told he will give us great endurance and patience that will ultimately allow us to share in the inheritance. Simple enough?

1 Thessalonians 5
15Make sure that nobody pays back wrong for wrong, but always try to be kind to each other and to everyone else.

If someone tells you to "make sure" you do something, is it a suggestion? Of course not, it's a firm directive, right? We Americans love to say, "Don't get mad, get even". There may not be another saying that runs so counter to the commandments of Jesus Christ, yet many, including Christians, love to quote this damaging remark regularly. As I write this in 2004, we are at war with Iraq largely because we're "getting even". Even though our government admits they have found no connection between Saddam Hussein and the attacks on the World Trade Center in 2001, we still went to war against Iraq. I read a poll this morning that reported Americans are increasingly withdrawing support for the war. While I appreciate the fact Americans are now reconsidering their position, it's a little too late at this stage. The President had overwhelming support at the time he announced the war, and for all the Americans who rallied around the President's decision, you'll need to ride out that decision until it runs its course. Sadly, I really doubt the average "Joe Sixpack" would think much differently the next time a situation like Iraq presents itself. We may have a chance to find out very soon.

2 Timothy 2
24And the Lord's servant must not quarrel; instead, he must be kind to everyone, able to teach, not resentful. 25Those who oppose him he must gently instruct, in the hope that God will grant them repentance leading them to a knowledge of the truth, 26and that they will come to their senses and escape from the trap of the devil, who has taken them captive to do his will.

Although I'm opposed to war, that doesn't make me a peaceful person. Perhaps my sin of impatience and lack of tolerance for other people makes God just as unhappy with my actions as those of the war-monger. I think the key in the passage above is that I can only hope that **"God will grant them repentance lead-ing them to a knowledge of the truth"**.

Hebrews 3
[14]**We have come to share in Christ if we hold firmly till the end the confi-dence we had at first.** [15]**As has just been said:**
   "Today, if you hear his voice,
      do not harden your hearts
   as you did in the rebellion."

The little word "if" is as big as an eighteen-wheeler in the passage above. **"We have come to share in Christ IF we hold firmly till the end the confidence we had at first."** How many Christians hear the Good News and proclaim they will live for Jesus, yet fade as the years pass?

Revelation 12
[17]**Then the dragon was enraged at the woman and went off to make war against the rest of her offspring—those who obey God's commandments and hold to the testimony of Jesus.**

If the "dragon" is Satan, who is his enemy? **"Those who obey God's command-ments and hold to the testimony of Jesus"**. If a person isn't opposed by Satan, then they need to reconsider the health of their Christianity. Satan won't bother anyone who isn't in his way, which I suppose might comfort some people, but those same people need to consider that Jesus subscribes to the thought, "You're either with me or against me".

Sometimes I find it difficult to accept that the Jesus in Revelation is the same Jesus of the Gospels. There seems to be a huge difference in the demeanor of the man from the beginning of the New Testament versus the end. Many modern Christians may not even be aware of the transformation from his quiet to fiery persona in Revelation, and that's a problem. If a Christian only knows about the gentle Savior from the Gospels, they only know half of the story. The meek and mild Savior invites us to "come, follow me", whereas the resurrected, conquering Savior warns, "it's time to fish or cut bait". The story has been told and is avail-able for all to hear. Satan, the "dragon" in the passage above will one day make war with those who don't already belong to him. Who are those people? Jesus tells us quite clearly: **"Those who obey God's commandments and hold to the testimony of Jesus"**.

Closing Thoughts

It's unusual for an author to finish a book with the comment, "I hope you haven't enjoyed this book", but that's exactly how I feel. If a person goes to his doctor and gets the diagnosis: "You have cancer", how often does the doctor finish up by saying, "I hope you've enjoyed what I've had to say". That's ridiculous, and it's just as foolish for me to write a book of this type and think people will walk away feeling good about their lives. I wrote this book to remind myself of God's instructions, and if someone else out there sees themselves in some of the examples I've written about, that's simply icing on the cake. The Scriptural passages in this book are like the diagnosis from the doctor—you can get mad and you can reject the information, but if the news is accurate, you'll have to deal with it sooner or later. As I stated in the foreword, I don't have all the answers. Some of my comments will be taken to task by people much smarter than I, but one thing remains: The Scriptures. If you've read this book and take issue with what I say, that's fine. Now go back and read only the Scriptural references and decide if your life in is alignment with God's word.

978-0-595-35154
0-595-35154-9

Made in the USA
Coppell, TX
14 September 2021

62376333R00062